BOKOTOLA

BOKOTOLA

Millard Fuller

Association Press
𝒻 **Follett Publishing Company/Chicago**

BOKOTOLA

Published by Association Press, 291 Broadway, New York, N.Y. 10007

Library of Congress Catalog Card Number: 78-3145
International Standard Book Number: 0-695-81179-7

23456789/838281807978

Library of Congress Cataloging in Publication

Fuller, Millard, 1935-
    Bokotola.
    1. Missions–Zaire. 2. Labor and laboring classes–Dwellings–Zaire. 3. Fuller, Millard, 1935- 4. Missionaries–Zaire–Biography.
    I. Title.
BV3625.C6F8   266'.0096751   77-1277
ISBN 0-8096-1924-5 pbk.
Third Printing, 1978

PRINTED IN THE UNITED STATES OF AMERICA

CONTENTS

Acknowledgments

IN a real sense, this book was not written; it happened. I was simply the one to begin recording it. The first writing took place, beginning in 1973, in correspondence and newsletters to friends and partners at home about the work in Zaire. Early in 1976, when letters arrived from several interested people in almost as many days suggesting a book about the project, I decided to think seriously about pulling everything together in an orderly manuscript.

My wife Linda plunged in to help me by searching through dozens of letter files to locate the best description of each episode and then organizing the material as I needed it. She wrote some sections herself, including the entire chapter about Mbandaka.

When I was halfway through the first draft I sent a chapter to Diane Scott in Salem, New Jersey, a longtime friend and partner in the work at Koinonia Farm in Georgia, and in Zaire. I knew that she was a capable writer who had published a number of poems and articles; I asked her opinion of the material, and whether she would be willing to help put it into shape to publish.

What I didn't know was that Diane, a working partner with her husband, Vic, in their wholesale nursery business, Colonial Nurseries, Inc., had just been asking the Lord for a job that would use her abilities as a writer. He answered her prayer by dumping on her desk a manuscript that required seven months of concentrated effort to organize, edit, and rewrite. And all this at the fantastic salary of "Serving the Lord with Gladness!"

When Diane needed help with retyping, she prayed about that, too. The answer came in the person of a friend and neighbor, Jean Johnson, who spent many hours at the typewriter (and got paid at the same rate). Diane's daughter Ellen did some typing too, along with my Aunt Irene Meadows in Fairfax, Alabama.

To all of these people, and especially to Diane, my deepest appreciation for their tremendous contribution. To them and to everyone else in Zaire, the United States, and Canada who has helped to give flesh and blood to the unfolding dream, I dedicate this book.

MILLARD FULLER

Koinonia Farm
January, 1977

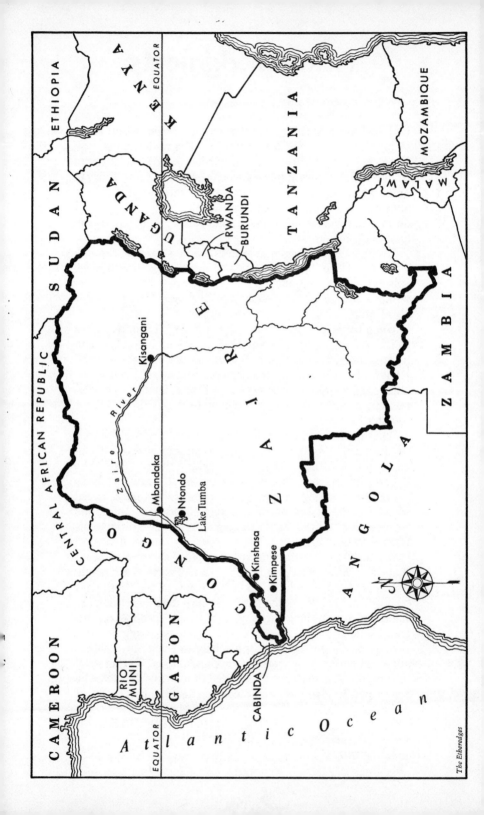

1
Beginnings

I SUPPOSE my interest in providing decent housing for poor people could be traced to Montgomery, Alabama, when I was in business there. We had a janitor in the company who spoke to me repeatedly about his need for a decent house for his family. I liked Lessie and looked for some way to help him. When our company bought a new office building, I discovered there was on the same lot an adjacent dwelling that had to be moved. I located a lot suitable for a residence a few miles out of town, engaged a house-moving gang, and we jacked that house up, put it on a truck, and rolled off down the road. Within a few days we had painted the house, repaired the little damage done in moving, and Lessie and his young family moved in. I recall vividly what a great joy it was to see them happily living in a decent place.

A couple of years later, cataclysmic changes occurred in my life, precipitated by a crisis in my marriage. The upshot was that my wife Linda and I decided together to change our lives from a business, success, get-richer orientation to one of seeking to serve in Christ's name.

I had been involved in the world of commerce since I was six years old, when my dad, who ran a small grocery store on the edge of the cotton-mill town of Lanett, Alabama, had bought me a pig. My instructions were to fatten him up, sell him, and make myself some money. That I did—and I enjoyed the experience of being a successful businessman. More pigs followed; then chickens and rabbits; and a small enterprise in firecrackers.

When I was about twelve years old, my father bought a farm. I decided to sell my assets and invest in cattle. Until my senior year in high school I was in the cattle business, and that income paid my way through college at nearby Auburn University.

Later, as a law student at the University of Alabama, I launched a series of business ventures with a fellow student, Morris Dees. Our enterprises included student apartment-house rentals, fancy birthday cakes, student telephone directories and desk blotters, and a mail-order business offering products such as holly wreaths, door mats and trash-can hold-

ers to youth groups throughout the country for fund raising.
The businesses blossomed, and by Commencement Day we
were making $50,000 a year—and we questioned the wisdom
of graduating!

Morris and I moved to Montgomery and opened our law
practice, continuing to launch new business ventures as The
Fuller and Dees Marketing Group, Inc. The Group eventually
included a dozen subsidiary corporations. The University-re-
lated deals were dropped, but we expanded mail-order selling
to youth groups. Tractor cushions were sold to Future Farm-
ers of America chapters for fund raising. Five new Ford trac-
tors were offered as prizes to the top selling groups, and
within three months we had sold 20 freight-car loads of
cushions at a $70,000 net profit.

Next, we published a cookbook and offered it to Future
Homemakers of America chapters for fund raising. Within a
few months we were selling cookbooks by the thousands and
making a handsome profit. In two years our company had
published cookbooks as fund raisers for many organizations,
and we found ourselves the largest publisher of cookbooks in
the world. Next came toothbrushes and candy, and other kinds
of publishing ventures.

Eight years after our first undertaking at the University,
we owned a plush, modern office building in Montgomery with
our names emblazoned across the top of it; we employed 150
people, including a battery of secretaries; and our sales were
over three million dollars a year. As president of the company,
my annual salary was $100,000.

One day in 1964, I was sitting in my office when the treasurer of our companies came bounding in and tossed a stack of
papers on my desk.

"Congratulations," she exclaimed. "You are a millionaire!"

"A millionaire? Let me see those papers!"

It was true. Financial statements had just been completed
on all the corporations in the Fuller and Dees Marketing
Group as well as personal statements for me and for my partner. We had reached the goal so many strive for: a million-
dollar financial statement for each of us.

I looked up at the treasurer, a bright, pretty young woman
who had started working with us right after our graduation
from law school. She had watched from the inside the rapid
rise of our enterprises, and she took a great personal interest
in the company.

"Congratulations, Millard." She said it again as she stood
there beaming at me from the other side of the desk. "What is
your next goal?"

"My next goal? Why, ten million! Why not?"

"Okay," she replied. "Why not?"

"Good. Since we agree, get back out there and go to work on it. Time's a-wastin'!"

With that, she shuffled the statements together, bundled them up in her arms, and hurried out of the office.

I pushed my chair back from the desk and spent a few minutes thinking over the past. In a very short time, I had amassed a fortune, with all the trimmings. We lived in a beautiful house in the Cloverdale section of Montgomery; plans were already being drawn for a $100,000 mansion to be built on a 20-acre lot I had recently bought at the edge of the city. I was driving a brand-new Lincoln Continental; on nearby Lake Jordan we had a lovely week-end home, complete with two speedboats. Out in the country, my partner and I owned three farms, totaling 2,000 acres, with hundreds of cattle, saddle horses, and numerous fishing lakes. And of course there was the business, making money at an ever-increasing rate. I had much to be proud of—possessions, prestige, and prospects for more of the same.

But my life was a thunderstorm about to break. Although I was less than thirty years old, I could not breathe properly. The pressures were so great that several times a day I would grasp the arms of my chair, pushing myself up and gasping desperately for breath. A big sore had developed on my left ankle and would not heal—doctors told me it was nervousness. The close and loving relationship I enjoyed with Linda had cooled to the point where we shared very little except our king-sized bed. We had everything—successful business, cattle ranch, cabin on the lake, speedboats, expensive clothes, Lincoln Continental, big house, and plans for a mansion. But deep in the recesses of my mind I was beginning to wonder: Is more and more of this to be the sum total of my life? Am I really devoting myself to the things God intended for me?

I had been raised in a Christian family and had been taught from earliest childhood the precepts of the Christian faith. I had embraced it. Accepted it. Was baptized. "Seek ye first the Kingdom of God, and all else shall be added." I believed that, and tried to live by it.

In high school and college, I had been active in youth affairs of our church. I was elected president of the youth organization of the Southeast Conference of Congregational Christian Churches—United Church of Christ (this included churches in Kentucky, Tennessee, Alabama, Georgia, South Carolina and Florida), and I had served in that capacity for three years. I participated in national youth conferences at Yale University, Doane College in Crete, Nebraska, and Catawba College in Salisbury, North Carolina. At Doane Conference I had been a candidate for national president of the Youth Group.

In more recent years, I had remained active in the church. In Montgomery, I had organized a new church in our home. I became president of the laymen's organization for the same Southeast Conference I had served as youth president a few years previously.

But, as business demanded more and more of my time, I sensed that my interest in the church was declining. One day in 1964, not long after receiving the million-dollar financial statement from our company treasurer, I received a letter from the national Stewardship Council of the church. They wanted me to visit a number of African missions, studying them from a layman's point of view, and then return to the States as a resource person to interpret the work to congregations and conferences.

My first impulse was to accept, but as I reflected more I decided I couldn't afford to. The business was growing rapidly. My whole mind was wrapped up in it. Could I step out of the action completely for a month or two and go traipsing all over Africa visiting missionaries? I took out a pad and pencil and did a bit of quick figuring on the cost of such a jaunt. Not the cost of airplane tickets, food, lodging, etc.—all that was nothing. I figured the cost of being away from the business, the loss of potential income and profits. That expense, I calculated, was too high. I said No.

"Seek ye first the Kingdom of God, and all else shall be added." Was I abandoning that fundamental precept of Christian life? The nagging question kept returning. A Christian is not to count the cost of following Christ, but I had counted the cost, and it was too high. All that can come later, I reasoned, *after* I've secured my fortune. Now is the time to make it, and store it up. Later, I'll have more time and money to give and then I'll put the Kingdom first. With all my strength I pushed questions of conscience back into the deepest, darkest corners of my mind. Still, I couldn't completely smother them.

In November of 1965, Linda brought the whole matter to the crisis point when she suddenly and firmly announced one evening that she had decided to go to New York to think about the future of our marriage. When she had gone, leaving me with our two young children, Chris and Kim, the rumbling thunderstorm within me began to roil. I was in agony. Never before or since have I suffered as I did during those days. Everything else—business, sales, profits, prestige, everything which had seemed so important—paled into total meaninglessness.

I began to examine my life and to ask what it was all about. An image came into my mind of the day I would stand before the Judge of History and have Him ask me what I had done with my life. I could hear myself squeaking, "Lord, I sold a hell of a lot of cookbooks." In the presence of God that sounded so ridiculous I could only cringe.

After a week of misery I could sit still no longer. I asked a pilot in our company to arrange for an airplane to go on a trip.

"Where to?" he inquired.

"I think I'll go to Niagara Falls," I replied.

"But why?"

"Because I've never been there!"

"Okay. It's your money!"

As we were coming into the Niagara Falls airport in the early evening, we went into a cloud bank. We lost radio contact with the tower, and the wings were icing up. The plane began to lose altitude. Just at that moment the radio crackled and we heard the tower yelling, "Look out! Look out! Plane coming right under you!"

We thought we were done for. Suddenly we broke out of the cloud and saw the lights of the city of Niagara Falls spread out like a fairyland below us. We sailed in for a smooth, uneventful landing, but the whole episode was not exactly soothing to my already shaken psyche.

We took a taxi and drove to the Canadian side to find a hotel for the night. As we dressed for dinner in our room, Jim, the pilot, flipped on the television set. The program, just starting, featured a young woman who had gone to China as a missionary. After a few years there she fell in love with a young Chinese military officer. He loved her and wanted to marry her, but he knew it would probably mean the end of his military career. He went to an old village leader—a mandarin—to ask for advice. The old man thought for a moment, and then replied, "A planned life can only be *endured*."

Those words penetrated my innermost being. "A planned life." That's what I'm living, I thought. And I'm enduring it and suffering. My plan was simply to get richer and richer, to make the company bigger and bigger, to acquire more and more things. Finally I would be buried in the rich section of the Montgomery cemetery.

"A planned life can only be *endured*."

With those words ringing in my ears, I phoned Linda and persuaded her to let me come to New York to talk to her. The following day Jim flew me to Watervliet, New York, to see one of our suppliers of tooth brushes, and from there to La Guardia airport in New York City. Jim then took the plane back to Montgomery, leaving me to go to Linda.

She had been counseling with Dr. Lawrence Durgin, pastor of the Broadway United Church of Christ. We had both met Dr. Durgin a couple of years earlier when we had lived briefly in New York City. Linda had been impressed with him and had decided to seek his advice rather than that of someone in our home area. As we talked, Linda described her counseling sessions, but confessed that she had not arrived at a decision about our marriage.

That evening we decided to go to Radio City Music Hall. The movie was entitled "Never Too Late." What a prophetic title, I thought! It is never too late to come back from a wrong turn, to correct a broken relationship with another person, or with God. But how?

After the movie (which was, incidentally, a very funny comedy about a woman who got pregnant after she thought it was too late!), we went downstairs for refreshments while we waited for the stage show. As we were sipping orange juice, Linda suddenly broke down and began crying. I couldn't get her to stop. Finally, in exasperation, I grabbed our coats and we stumbled out into the cold November night, leaving the stage show, the orange juice, and an umbrella!

We walked around for a while just holding on to each other while Linda's sobs subsided. We sat down on the front steps of St. Patrick's Cathedral and talked. Then we walked some more, eventually ending up in the doorway of a shop just off Fifth Avenue. There it happened. Linda faced me and bared her soul. She confessed the ways in which she had betrayed our relationship. I poured out my own agony and regret for ways I had betrayed her. The wall was broken down, and love rushed in like a mighty flood. We grabbed each other and held on as the tears flowed down our cheeks.

After a long while we took a taxi and returned to our hotel. We stayed up all night talking, singing, and praying. The song that came to us was "We're Marching to Zion." That tune absolutely filled my heart and soul. I couldn't stop singing it. (We were still singing it three days later, on the plane to Montgomery, cheerfully ignoring the stares of our fellow passengers!)

> We're marching to Zion,
> Beautiful, beautiful Zion;
> We're marching upward to Zion,
> The beautiful city of God.
>
> Come, we that love the Lord,
> And let our joys be known,
> Join in a song with sweet accord,
> Join in a song with sweet accord,

And thus surround the throne,
And thus surround the throne.

We both felt a strong sense of God's presence as we talked about the future. We felt that God was calling us out of this situation to a new life, a new way of walking. To prepare for this new thing—whatever it was—we felt it necessary to leave the business, sell our interest in it, and give away all the proceeds.

The following morning we left our room and went downstairs to go somewhere—I've forgotten where. I hailed a taxi, and we crawled in. But the driver didn't drive off. Instead, he turned around to us with a big smile on his face.

"Congratulations!"

"Congratulations? For what?" I asked.

"This is a brand-new taxi. You are my first passengers!"

I turned to Linda. She was already crying.

"Driver," I said, "take us on a drive through Central Park. I've got a story to tell you."

As we wound our way through the park I leaned my arms on the back of the driver's seat and shared with him what we had experienced the night before and how we had decided to change our lives and serve God. He was deeply moved, and felt, as we did, that his picking us up that morning was a sign from God that we had made the right decision.

Two days later we experienced another powerful and moving sign. We were at Kennedy airport waiting to take the plane to Montgomery. As we sat in the waiting area, a young African in long, flowing robes took a seat near us. Linda and I had already been talking about the possibility of going to Africa to see how we might relate to needs there, so we were interested in this young man.

I whispered to Linda, "I'd like to talk to him."

"Well," she said, "go over and introduce yourself and start talking!"

Suiting action to words, I walked over and tried a tentative "Hello."

"Hello," he responded, in crisp British English.

I introduced myself and we began to chat. He told me he had just arrived from Nigeria, that he was on his way to Birmingham, Alabama, to study at Miles College there, and that I was the first American to greet and talk to him. His name was Daniel Offiong.

Meanwhile, the flight was announced, and we all scrambled

to board the plane. Inside we had assigned seats. When everyone had been seated, we turned to discover that my new friend was right behind us. There were two empty seats beside him, so when the plane was airborne we moved back and continued our conversation.

Daniel told us many things about himself and his aspirations. He was the first young man from his tribe to go beyond high school, and everyone back home was putting their hopes on him. He did not want to disappoint them—especially his family, who had sacrificed so much to further his education. He explained that his mission church had obtained a tuition scholarship for him at Miles College, but that he would be responsible for getting the money for other expenses.

I asked him how much money he had. He pulled out a packet of traveler's checks and handed them to me.

"Here's my money," he said. "Is it much?"

I counted it. There were eight $10 traveler's checks.

"Is that all?" I asked.

"Yes, that's all."

Realizing that he didn't know anything about the value of American money, I gave him a short course on nickels, dimes, quarters, half dollars, and dollars, and the value of each in terms of purchasing power. It began to dawn on him that he had very little money! I asked if he had warm clothing for the winter. That morning it had been only nine degrees above zero in New York.

"No," he replied, "I only have clothing such as we wear in Nigeria."

I turned to Linda and asked if she had a checkbook in her purse. When she replied that she did, I told her to write out a $50 check for Daniel. At least he could get himself a decent coat when he arrived in Birmingham. I handed the check to him and explained that Linda and I wanted to give it to him as a gesture of help and encouragement and specifically to buy himself a coat when he arrived·in Birmingham. He accepted the check and gazed at it for a long moment. Then tears welled up in his eyes. He unbuckled his seat belt, stood up, and bowed deeply to both of us. Then he sat down again, continuing to gaze at the check.

"I'd like to tell you a story," he said. "Yesterday, before going to the airport, I went to say goodbye to my pastor. When I arrived at his house he was with a group of Christians in a prayer meeting. They asked me to kneel and all of them laid hands on me and asked God's blessings on me. When the prayer ended I stood up and the pastor put his arms around me and said, 'Daniel, I have a prophecy to make. When you reach America tomorrow, you will meet a good Samaritan who will help you and see you through your needs there'." Daniel looked at us and said through his tears, "Now this prophecy has come true."

A few months later I told this story in Marble Collegiate Church in New York City. A young woman, a native of Mississippi, was in the audience. After the service she came up and told me how much she was moved, and that she wanted to help. As a result of her efforts, a Daniel Offiong Scholarship was established at Tougaloo College in Jackson, Mississippi. (Daniel had transferred to Tougaloo, a small, predominantly black school related to the United Church of Christ and the Christian Church [Disciples of Christ]. This scholarship provided for his needs during his college years and continues to provide $1,000 a year there for some needy student. Daniel had a brilliant college career, eventually receiving his doctorate degree.)

In the weeks that followed we sold our business interests and properties; set in motion the process of giving away our assets; spent a month at Koinonia Farm in Georgia, talking, thinking, and praying about the future God had for us; and contacted the United Church Board for World Ministries about the trip through Africa that had been suggested a year earlier.

That trip took place in the summer of 1966. Linda and I spent two months visiting schools, hospitals, self-help projects, and refugee programs of many denominations in Ghana, Tanzania, Rhodesia, South Africa, and Zaire (then known as Democratic Republic of Congo).

When we came to Mbandaka, the capital city of Equator Region in Zaire, Disciples missionaries showed us various kinds of ministries. One was a Block and Sand Project just purchased from a Belgian businessman who had fled the country at independence in 1960. The missionaries were excited about what they might accomplish with this operation. The housing situation was critical because of the flood of people coming into the city following repeal of the "influx control" laws that had prohibited large-scale migration to the cities in colonial days. As we drove around the dusty streets of Mbandaka looking at thousands of mud shacks and incredible living conditions, I wondered what we could do to help.

We didn't do much right away, except to give money for a new dump truck for the Block and Sand Project, but we couldn't get the need and the opportunity out of our heads.

* * *

For nearly two years after our African trip I traveled extensively throughout the United States speaking to churches, conferences, schools, and retreats, trying to awaken and sensitize people to the tremendous needs in countries like Tanzania, Ghana, and Zaire. Also, at this time I opened an office in New York City to launch a $10 million fund drive for Tougaloo College.

Soon after I had established this New York office, I decided to call an old business and party buddy, Gene Gilbert, and arrange a visit. I had formerly had an office in his suite in the Pfizer Building near the United Nations, on 42nd Street. We had wheeled and dealed during the day and then lived it up at night. He lived in a fashionable apartment on the East Side, on 72nd Street. One night he threw a big party complete with Arabian belly dancers and top musician Herbie Mann. Even though his apartment was on the top floor—a penthouse—we made so much noise that the police were called to calm the place down.

I liked Gene. We had made money together and we raised cain together, but that was the extent of our relationship. I had never once shared anything with him about my Christian faith. Now I wanted to see him again. But what in the world would I tell him? What would he think of me, out of business, working for a Negro college, and talking about the Lord? For days I hesitated. Then, late one Friday afternoon, I had such a tremendous urge to contact him that I could not resist it. I phoned him. His office was still in the Pfizer Building, while mine was on Broadway and 56th, in the old Broadway Church pastored by our friend Dr. Durgin.

"Hello, Gene."

"Millard Fuller! Where are you?"

"I'm in New York, man."

"Well, get over here right now."

I hesitated again, pleading that it was too late in the day. Tomorrow, I said . . . or next week. But he insisted that I come *right that minute!*

I rode over on the subway, wondering what I was going to say to him. I knew he would ask a hundred questions—about business, about how much money I was making, about what kind of new deals I had going. I kept praying, "Lord, fill me with your words."

When I got to his office, sure enough, Gene started right in asking about the company, profits and so on. He fired questions so fast I couldn't answer them. Finally, he paused, and I leaned forward: "Gene," I said, "I'm no longer in business, and I want to tell you about it."

He was shocked. "What deal went wrong?"

"No business deal went wrong," I replied, "but there were a lot of other things that were wrong."

He sensed I had something serious to say, and he settled back in his chair. For perhaps thirty minutes I poured out my heart to him, telling him of my personal problems and of the decision Linda and I had made right there in New York to give up the business and our possessions, and to devote our lives to serving Christ.

When I finished speaking, he leaned forward and looked me straight in the eyes. "Millard," he said, "you don't know what today is, do you?"

"No," I answered. "What do you mean?"

"Today is my fortieth birthday, and I want you to know that you have just given me the best birthday present of my life."

Later, he drove me back to my apartment, asking, probing, and yearning to know everything I had experienced. As he stopped his car in front of our building, he told me he wanted me to come to his place and share what I had told him with his wife. Although he had not been married when I had last seen him, I happened to know the girl he had married.

A couple of nights later Linda and I went to their apartment for dinner. Gene's wife, Nancy, met us at the door. "What have you been telling my husband?" she blurted out, as soon as the door opened.

"Why, hello, Nancy. What do you mean?"

"What have you been telling my husband, Millard Fuller? I'm afraid he is going to give our money away!"

She was smiling and friendly, but we could sense a note of concern in her voice, too. She ushered us into their luxurious living room. Another invited guest was already there, an executive of a large corporation.

As we took our seats, Gene burst into the room in his usual exuberant way.

"Millard, tell them what you told me the other day. I want Nancy and my friend to hear that story."

I turned to them and started to speak, but Gene interrupted me before I had completed the first sentence.

"No, wait," he said, "I'll tell them."

And he began recounting exactly what I had told him. He remembered everything. I was amazed. He concluded by saying that he had never been so moved by anything, and that he felt he must now take some action in response, but he didn't yet know what he should do.

The reaction of his listeners was instant and totally negative. "Millard, you've gone nuts," they chimed together.

"No," Gene responded. "He has not gone nuts. *We* are nuts."

But they wouldn't be moved. Nancy was a secular woman with no association with any religious group or organization. The man was a nominal Catholic. Both were content with their lives and saw no need for a religion that made demands on them. Gene, like his wife, had been a totally secular person, but now he saw something else, and he felt compelled from within to deal with his new awakening.

Every day after that Gene called me to talk, to ask questions, to seek. He wanted to get together again and talk some more. We set a date, but he called back to say that he had to go to Washington and couldn't make it.

The following Sunday Linda and I went to church. When we walked back into the lobby of our apartment building, the boy on the desk called to me with a telephone message. It was from Nancy, Gene's wife.

I went upstairs and phoned her. When she picked up the phone and I spoke to her, she started crying.

"Nancy," I inquired anxiously, "what is wrong?"

"Millard, come over here as quickly as you can."

"Yes, I will, but why?"

"Just a few minutes ago Gene dropped dead. A heart attack."

I ran downstairs and hailed a taxi. All the way over I kept thinking about what this meant.Gene had been the picture of health and energy, deeply tanned from a recent cruise in the Caribbean, the president of a successful corporation. Now he was dead.

As soon as I reached the apartment Nancy called me into a side room where she sat down. "Millard, tell me, why has this happened? We have many friends, but you are the only one who ever talks about religion."

In the long minutes that followed, I shared with her, as I had earlier with Gene, my personal experiences with the Lord. Among other things, I told her that I believed God had sent me to Gene to talk to him about God. His heart had been open and he had gladly received the message. I told her there were many mysteries in life that could not be fully understood, but that we should simply accept the fact of God, and of His love. We know that this love is constantly available, and we should desire it, seek after it. Gene, I said, was now in God's care, and, knowing that He is love, we should not worry.

On the day of Gene's funeral, I gave Nancy a Bible in which I had written about the feelings Gene and I had shared just days before his sudden death. She gladly accepted the Bible and said she would always treasure it. It was the only one she had.

I have lost track of Nancy in the years since then, and I have often wondered about her. I do know, however, that at that time, she and Gene, like Daniel Offiong and the taxi driver, contributed valuable pieces to the jumbled puzzle of my life which God was gradually helping me to put together.

2
Clarence Jordan

IN June of 1968, after two years of traveling, speaking, and fund raising, we felt God heading us in another direction. As a result, we returned to Americus, Georgia, to work with Clarence Jordan in establishing a new movement at Koinonia Farm.

This Christian communal farm (*Koinonia* is the Greek word for "fellowship," or "community") had been established in 1942 by Clarence and Florence Jordan and Martin and Mabel England. The Englands left soon thereafter, but the Jordans had stayed on to oversee the development of a thriving community. It had been all but destroyed, however, by Ku Klux Klan violence in the late 1950's and early 60's.

Koinonia was the object of hostility because of its uncompromising witness to the universal brotherhood of man and its practical commitment to the idea that in Christ "there is neither Jew nor Greek, there is neither bond nor free, there is neither male nor female; for you are all one in Christ Jesus."

Blacks and whites lived and worked together at Koinonia in a spirit of Christian brotherhood. This enraged many of the white segregationists in the surrounding area, and eventually they set upon the community with a vengeance—beatings, bombings, burnings, and a total economic boycott. The fact that even a remnant of the community survived is a miracle.

By 1968 the two remaining families were seriously considering giving up. Then a new direction for Koinonia began to emerge. Clarence talked about this in an open letter written in October of 1968:

TO FRIENDS OF KOINONIA

For several years it has been clear that Koinonia stands at the end of an era or perhaps of its existence. Its goals and methods which were logical and effective in the 1940's and 50's seem no longer relative to an age which is undergoing vast and rapid changes. An integrated Christian community was a very practical vehicle through which to witness to a segregated society a decade ago, but now it is too slow, too weak, not aggressive enough. Its lack of mobility gives it the appearance of a house on the bank of a river as the rushing torrents of history swirl by.

The obvious answer was to call it quits. The group had already dwindled to a mere handful—two families, to be exact. About a year ago, Florence and I decided that we would seek other directions, and friends extended invitations to join faculties, to pastor churches, to be this-and-that-in-residence, etc.

But somehow nothing seemed to click. Perhaps I was suffering from "battle fatigue." It was as though I were living in a spiritual vacuum. No joy, no excitement, no sense of mission.

In this state of torpor, I got a very brief note from Millard Fuller, whom I had met in December of 1965 when he and his family stopped at Koinonia to visit for a half hour with his friend Al Henry. As the half hour stretched into a day and finally into a month, we learned that this was a time of deep spiritual crisis for Millard and his wife, Linda, and that both had reached the brink of destruction. Millard had become a "money addict" and was more enslaved to it than any alcoholic to his bottle. He had already become a millionaire and was reaching for more.

But God reached for him, turned him around, and gave him the wisdom to do what even the rich young ruler in the Bible wouldn't do—"Go, sell what thou hast and give it to the poor, and come, follow me."

During his month here, Millard transacted by phone much of the business necessary to liquidate his assets in Montgomery, Alabama, and to distribute them to charitable purposes. Being a white native of Alabama, Millard wanted to express his discipleship to Christ in service to blacks. He got a job raising money for Tougaloo College, a Negro school near Jackson, Mississippi. In this he was both happy and successful.

His note to me in May of this year was brief and direct. "I have just resigned my job with Tougaloo. What have you got up your sleeve?"

Nothing up my sleeve, or in my head or heart, I'm blank.

But wait a minute. Does God have something up *His* sleeve—for both of us? I got on the phone and called Millard at his New York office. Could God be trying to say something to us, to accomplish some purpose through us?

We decided to get together at once and discuss it. I would be preaching in a few days at the Oakhurst Baptist Church in Atlanta, and we decided to meet there. At the end of a long day of discussion and prayer, both of us were convinced that God had given a radically new direction to our lives.

We still cannot fully articulate this leading of God's spirit. But we have the deep feeling that modern man's greatest problems stem from his loss of any sense of meaningful participation with God in His purposes for mankind. For most people God really and truly is dead, stone dead.

With no upward reach, no sense of partnership with God, man has chosen to be a loner, trying to solve on his own, but always in deep frustration and desperation, crushing problems which increasingly threaten to destroy him. But from bitter experience, beginning at the Tower of Babel, we should know by now that "unless the Lord builds the house, those who build it labor in vain."

The church has been saying this all along—without believing its own message. So it has thrown up its hands and joined the multitudes who look to the Government for salvation. But even with billions of dollars at its disposal, Government cannot give man a God-dimension to his life. It is inherently incapable of reaching the inner recesses of his being, which must be touched if life on this planet is to be even passingly tolerable.

It has also become clear to us that as man has lost his identity with God he has lost it with his fellow man. We compete with one another fiercely; we even want to kill human beings for whom Christ died. Our cities provide us anonymity, not community. Instead of partners, we are aliens and strangers.

As a result, the poor are being driven from rural areas; frustrated, angry masses huddle in the cities; suburbanites walk in fear; the chasm between blacks and whites grows wider; war hysteria invades every part of the earth.

We must have a new spirit—a spirit of partnership with one another.

But how does a dream become deed and a vision reality? Can lofty speculation be transformed into practical, hard-nosed action?

In mid-August of 1968, we called together fifteen spiritually sensitive and socially aware men of God for a four-day session of seeking, thinking, talking about these questions. They were businessmen, politicians, writers, ministers, free lancers—all with a deep compassion for their fellow men. From this conference emerged a course of action which we shall call Koinonia Partners. It will have three prongs: 1) Communication, 2) Instruction, 3) Application.

1. By *Communication* we mean the sowing of the seed, the spreading of the radical ideas of the gospel message; the call to faith in God and the reshaping and restructuring of our lives around His will and purpose. It means "to preach good news to the poor, to proclaim release to the captives and recovering of sight to the blind, to set at liberty those who are oppressed."

To do this we will use every available means of modern communication. We will travel and speak extensively across the land and throughout the world. We will make tapes, records, and films, publish books, and circulate literature in every way possible. Already a good start has been made in this direction, but it will be greatly intensified.

2. By *Instruction* we mean the constant teaching and training of the "partners" to enable them to become more effective and mature. There will be traveling "discipleship schools" to follow up and conserve the results of the speaking and communicating, to keep alive the new spirit, to strengthen and encourage. The first such school is already scheduled for early January of 1969.

3. *Application*, in its initial stages, will consist of *partnership industries, partnership farming*, and *partnership housing*. These will be implemented through a Fund for Humanity.

What the poor need is not charity but capital, not caseworkers but co-workers. And what the rich need is a wise, honorable and just way of divesting themselves of their overabundance. The Fund for Humanity will meet both of these needs.

Money for the Fund will come from shared gifts by those who feel that they have more than they need, from non-interest-bearing loans from those who cannot afford to make the gift but who do want to provide working capital for the disinherited, and from the voluntarily shared profits from the partnership industries, farms, and houses. As a starter, it has been agreed to transfer all of Koinonia Farm's assets of about $250,000 to the Fund. Other gifts are already beginning to come in.

The Fund will give away no money. It is not a handout. It will provide capital for the partnership enterprises.

The first enterprise to be launched is *partnership farming*. Under this plan all land will be held in trust by the Fund for Humanity, but will be used by the partners free of charge. Thus, usership will replace ownership. This can be done because the Fund's capital has been provided by those who care, and there is no need to pay interest on it.

The partners will be strongly encouraged, though not required, to contribute as liberally as possible to the Fund so as to keep enlarging it and making more capital available to others. As Jesus put it, "You have received it as a gift, so share it as a gift." If the partners have the right spirit (and I cannot see how this or any system can work without that) and there should be growing numbers—which it seems reasonable to predict—the Fund will be self-generative and ever-expanding.

The same principles will be applied to *partnership industries*. We already have a fairly flourishing pecan-shelling plant, fruitcake bakery, candy kitchen, and mail-order business. Once again, partners will operate these ventures with no capital outlay in the beginning and never any rent or interest.

Partnership housing is concerned with the idea that the urban ghetto is to a considerable extent the product of rural displacement. People don't move to the city unless life in the country has become intolerable; they do not voluntarily choose the degrading life in the big city slums. If land in the country is available on which to build a decent house, and if they can get jobs near by to support their families, they'll stay put.

So we have recently laid off 42 half-acre home sites and are making them available to displaced rural families. Four acres in the center are being reserved as a community park and recreational area. The Fund for Humanity will put up a four-bedroom house with bath, kitchen and living room, and this will be sold to a family over a twenty-year period with no interest, only a small monthly administration charge. Thus the cost will be about half the usual financing, and for a poor person this can be the difference between owning a house and not owning one. The interest forces him to pay for two houses but he gets only one.

As with farming and industries, the partner family will gradually free the initial capital to build houses for others, and will be encouraged to share at least a part of their savings on interest with the Fund for Humanity. Even as all are benefited, so should all share. If, as Jesus says, "it is more blessed to give than to get," then even the poorest should not be denied the extra blessedness of giving.

Perhaps I have now given you at least some understanding of Koinonia Partners and the new direction for my own life. I would like to encourage each of you to rethink your life and make whatever adjustments you feel necessary to bring it into line with the will of God.

Augustine once said, "He who possesses a surplus possesses the goods of others." That's a polite way of saying that anybody who has too much is a thief. If you are a "thief," perhaps you should set a reasonable living standard for your family and restore the "stolen goods" to humanity, either through the Fund or by some other suitable means. Some of you may wish to join us and seek the new life of partnership with God and man ...

Yours in Faith and expectation,
Clarence Jordan

Over the next four and a half years, Linda and I were engaged in turning the dream of Koinonia Partners and the Fund for Humanity into reality. For the first sixteen months I worked closely with Clarence. Often we met in his little "shack"—a simple one-room office out in the middle of a young pecan grove, a few hundred yards from the main complex of buildings.

Clarence's whole life was centered in God, and his single aim was constantly to seek His will and to be part of helping accomplish it on earth. He was God's partner in the fullest sense. For Clarence, the daily discovery of God's plan and the living of it was an exhilarating adventure. He spoke of the "God Movement" and of God's calling us to be a vital part of it. He wanted to be where God's action was. Faith, to him, was obedience—in scorn of the consequences.

Clarence was totally immersed in God's Word. His degree in agriculture from the University of Georgia prepared him to launch Koinonia Farm in the first place; but it was his Ph.D. in New Testament Greek from the Southern Baptist Seminary in Louisville, Kentucky, which enabled him to search the Scriptures so deeply.

Over a period of many years Clarence painstakingly translated portions of the New Testament into the "Cotton Patch" versions, which faithfully rendered the message and teachings of Christ in a contemporary American context. He said that nobody in the first century failed to understand Jesus' sermons—which was the cause of His problems—and Clarence wanted to make the Biblical imperatives just as stunningly clear to readers today.

Belief, Clarence taught, means "by-live," or "to live by." The thrust of the whole Bible, he pointed out, is from heaven earthward and not vice versa. God is trying to show us, through His Word, how to live *now*. Salvation is a present tense reality that affects our lives today, right where we are.

To repent, Clarence said, does not mean to feel sorry for getting caught, but it means complete change—"metamorphosis." He frequently compared this change to that of a caterpillar being transformed into a butterfly. True repentance, he continued, means a new life, a new set of values—a new creature in the Lord Jesus Christ.

To be with Clarence was a constantly stimulating experience. In 1965, when Linda and I first visited Koinonia, I had never heard of Clarence Jordan, and Koinonia was just a place where my friend Al Henry had moved a few months earlier. I knew nothing of Clarence's "Cotton Patch" translations, or that such a man of God lived so near our home in Alabama.

But God knew all this, and He led me to Clarence in my hour of greatest need. This man of tremendous depth and intellect, possessed of the keenest spiritual insights of any person I've ever known, lovingly nurtured me back to emotional and spiritual health when we were at the farm in December of that year. And again, in 1968, after our family had moved to Koinonia, he nurtured and taught me. We were friends and partners in a profound sense, and we reveled in being together in a venture with God.

Clarence and I both spoke widely throughout the country in those early months, putting into practice the Communications phase of Koinonia Partners. We conducted Discipleship Schools at Koinonia, and in New York and Indiana. In addition, Clarence resigned all his positions of responsibility in Koinonia Partners in order to devote his time to completing his "Cotton Patch" translations of the New Testament. A board of directors was chosen for the new Koinonia Partners organization.

Meanwhile, new people were pouring into Koinonia, and three hundred acres of adjoining farmland were purchased. An extensive partnership farming program was launched, the pecan-candy-fruitcake mail-order business was revitalized, and I got back into the cookbook business by promoting the Koinonia Pecan Cookbook! And we laid off the lots for the housing site and started building.

Within a year after announcing Koinonia Partners and the Fund for Humanity, we were well on the way to turning the dreams into reality.

Suddenly, one clear, crisp October afternoon in 1969, Clarence died. He was sitting at his desk in the isolated little shack he used as a study, preparing a talk to be given the next day at nearby Mercer University, when he had a heart attack. Lena Hofer, one of the many young people who had come to be a part of the dream of Koinonia Partners, was with him, having

stepped into the shack with a question just minutes earlier.
She dashed breathlessly into the Koinonia main office, yelling,
"Come quickly! Something is wrong with Clarence!"

His wife Florence and I ran out together, jumped into a car,
and raced the short distance down to the shack. When I
rushed in and saw him sitting there, with his head leaned back
against the wall, I knew instantly he was dead.

Sadness overwhelmed me, for this simple yet profound
farmer-preacher, in his faded blue jeans, plain cotton shirt,
and brogan boots, was my loved friend. But I was joyful, too. I
found myself muttering out loud, over and over, "You made it,
Clarence. You made it, friend. You made it."

We gathered up his body, put it into the vehicle, and took it
to his house in the community. I telephoned the county coroner
and requested that he come out and pronounce Clarence dead
so we could bury him. But the coroner would not come. Clarence, in his steadfast faithfulness to Christ, had refused to
compromise on the sensitive social issues, principally the race
question, and he had incurred the wrath of the power structure in that rural Southern county.

The coroner advised me that I must bring the body to the
hospital in town. So we loaded Clarence's body once again into
the farm station wagon, and I drove it to the hospital. There
we were kept waiting until nearly midnight while an examina-
tion and autopsy were performed, and an official pronounce-
ment was made that he was dead.

I drove the body back to the farm. The following afternoon
we buried Clarence in a pine grove on the back side of the farm
and, according to his wishes, in a homemade coffin. The poor
were there to honor him, and many others were there from
distant states, but no local church, community, or political
leaders came.

Before the funeral I went to Florence and asked her what
Scripture we should read at the service. She smiled and replied, "Read any of it, Millard. He loved it all."

But God gave me the Scripture. It summarized the basics of
the philosophy and religion of Clarence's life, and it will always
be special Scripture for me. It was taken from Clarence's
"Cotton Patch" translations of I John and I Peter.*

In order that you-all, too, might be our partners, we're plainly
telling you about something that's real, something that we ourselves
have heard, that we have seen with our own two eyes. ... The darkness is lifting and the true light is already dawning. Now a man who
claims to be in the light, but still hates his brother, is in the darkness
right on. The man who loves his brother lives in the light and has no
trick up his sleeve. But he who hates his brother is in the dark, lives

*The Cotton Patch version of Hebrews and the General Epistles, New York,
Association Press, 1973.

in the dark and has no idea what direction he's going, because the darkness has blindfolded him ...

Don't love the old order or the things which keep it going. If anyone loves the old order, it is not the Father's love that's in him. For everything that's in the old order—the hankering for physical comforts, the hankering for material things, the emphasis on status—is not from the Father but is from the old order itself. And the old order, with its hankerings, is collapsing, but he who lives by the will of God moves into the New Age ...

So don't be surprised, brothers, if the old order hates your guts. We ourselves are convinced that we have switched from death to life because we love the brothers. The man with no love still lives in death country ...

Loved ones, let's love each other, because love springs from God, and every lover has been fathered by God and is sensitive to God. The non-lover is not sensitive to God because God is love. And God's love took shape in our midst when he sent his one and only son into the world so we might start living. And that's real love—not that we loved God, but that he loved us and sent his son to answer for our wrongs. Loved ones, if God loved us that much, then we ought to love one another. Nobody has ever once caught a glimpse of God. Yet if we love everybody, God is present among us and his love is brought to maturity in us ...

Now that by your response to the truth you have dedicated your inner lives to genuine brother-love, go ahead and love one another straight from the heart with all you've got. For you all have been re-fathered, not by a mortal man, but by the immortal word of a living and abiding God.

> "Every human being is like a blade of grass.
> And his appearance is like a blossom.
> The grass dries up, the blossom falls off;
> But the Word of the Lord lives on and on."

After this Scripture, some songs and a prayer, we gathered around the simple grave and together lowered the box into the earth. Then, as we took shovels and started slowly, quietly, pushing the red Georgia clay into the grave, my two-year-old daughter, Faith, to the utter amazement of everyone, stepped to the edge and began to sing the only song she knew:

> "Happy birthday to you;
> Happy birthday to you;
> Happy birthday, dear Clarence;
> Happy birthday to you!"

I shall forever thank God for my friend and partner, Clarence, and the freshness of his spirit will abide in my heart always.

After Clarence's death we continued to realize the dream of

Koinonia. More people came, including Ladon Sheats, a former executive with the IBM Corporation, who had undergone a dramatic metamorphosis in his own life. He joined me in the speaking and teaching ministry of Koinonia Partners.

In the Application phase of the work, Linda started a handcrafts shop, which blossomed into a thriving mail-order business providing employment for several local women. A related sewing industry came next which developed into a production-line operation turning out thousands of pairs of women's slacks and giving jobs to more local poor people. A pottery was launched. We even started a partnership *worm* farm, selling worms to organic gardeners and fishermen by mail.

In the housing project, the original site Clarence had written about back in October of 1968 was completed, along with the community park, and a second site was selected. By mid-1972 this work and other phases of Koinonia's various ministries were running smoothly ... and I was restless to do something else.

"I wonder what is going on in that Block and Sand Project out in Zaire?" Linda didn't answer, because I was half talking to myself. "I wonder if we could start a Fund for Humanity there and do a housing project?

"Maybe. Yeah, maybe. But how do we get out there? And how do we live? We don't have any money, remember?"

"Maybe the Disciples will sponsor us."

Linda and I were sitting in a little motel room in Tallahassee, Florida. We had driven down there for the sole purpose of thinking through what we should do next, and trying to sense where God was now directing us.

"Why not call Bob Nelson?" (Dr. Robert Nelson is the Africa Secretary for the Christian Church [Disciples of Christ]. It was he who had arranged our visit in Zaire in 1966.)

"That's a good idea. I'll put in a call right now."

I picked up the telephone from its stand by the bed and dialed long distance. Within minutes I had Dr. Nelson on the line.

"Millard Fuller! I haven't heard from you in ages. How are you?"

After sharing a few pleasantries, I told Dr. Nelson the purpose of our call. We wanted to know whether the church in Zaire would like us to come out for a tour of service to help with development, and especially with the Block and Sand Project we had seen when we visited there ... and whether the Disciples would be willing to sponsor us.

"Millard," he replied, "your call is providential. If you had called two days ago I would have said No, but only yesterday a representative of the Zaire church was in my office asking for someone to help them with development. I told them we didn't have anyone—but now I can tell them we do!"

Dr. Nelson went on to add that of course he would have to go through normal channels for approval of the appointment, but he anticipated no problems. Nor did we. For once again God had given us a clear sign.

A visit was arranged to the Indianapolis headquarters of the Disciples Church. Procedures were set in motion, and we began planning a new life in the heart of Africa.

3
Preparations

"Un, deux, trois, quatre, cinq. Linda, guess what? I can count up to five now! Listen . . ."

The first task ahead of us was to learn French, the official language of Zaire. We knew from our earlier visit that practically no one out there spoke English.

We started our French studies at Koinonia with a basic course of books and records. Day and night we listened and repeated, listened and repeated.

"Peu."

"Peu? I don't know. This stuff is too hard. The French language is ridiculous."

"Peu, peu, peu. It means 'little.' Got that? *Peu.* 'Little'."

"Je parle très peu le français. (I speak very little French.)" ·

"That's for sure. I wonder if I'll ever speak more than a very little."

"Un, deux, trois, quatre, cinq, six, sept, huit, neuf, dix. Linda, I can count up to ten!"

It was a grueling, frustrating experience, but we stuck with it. By the time we left Koinonia in January of 1973, we could speak a few sentences.

Now began the next phase of our preparations—learning more about the country of Zaire. It was arranged for us to spend three months at the missionary orientation center in Stony Point, New York. There, in a marvelously quiet atmosphere, with a big missionary library at our disposal, we began intensive study of the area which would soon be our home.

Zaire is a large country in the middle of Africa, straddling the equator. In black Africa, only the Sudan has a larger land mass. With nearly a million square miles, it is the size of the United States east of the Mississippi River. But in population it is small. New York City and its environs contain more people than the entire country of Zaire. The dominating geographic influence of Zaire is the gigantic Zaire River, which with its tributaries totals 9,965 miles and forms the basis of the transportation system. It also provides countless tons of fish, a vital source of protein in an improverished country.

Zaire contains great mineral resources—and some of the poorest people on earth. Garbage collectors in New York City make more money every two weeks than a schoolteacher in

26

Zaire makes in a year. Only one million people out of the total population of twenty-three million are regularly employed.

For twenty-four years the country was the personal property of one man—King Leopold of Belgium. The famous explorer, Henry Morton Stanley, staked it out for him. King Leopold was officially awarded his prize by the Berlin Conference in 1885, which divided up the continent of Africa among European interests. Leopold surrendered his big estate (never having set foot on it) only after horrible atrocities committed by his agents came to light. In 1904 other European countries, and finally his own government, pressed him to relinquish control to the Belgian Government, which he did in 1908. It is estimated that while Leopold owned the Congo the population was reduced by several *million* people.

Virtually the whole known history of the Belgian Congo (now Zaire) has been one of cruelty, exploitation, and suffering. Stanley recorded a typical sacrifice of life at Equator Station in 1884 (present-day Mbandaka, where we would be living!):

An important chief of the neighbourhood—an old and long-ago superannuated potentate, of whose existence I had previously been unaware—died, and according to the custom of the By-Yanzi and Bakuti, slaves had to be massacred to accompany him to the land of spirits. Accordingly the relatives and freemen began to collect as many slaves as could be purchased. ... The mourning relatives secured fourteen men from the interior. ... The captives were despatched one after another. Their heads were unfleshed by boiling, that the skulls might decorate the poles round the grave. The bodies were dragged away and thrown into the Congo; the soil saturated with the blood was gathered up and buried with the defunct chief. (From *The Congo and the Founding of Its Free State*, by Henry M. Stanley, Vol. II, page 180.)

Such cruelty was commonplace. When Stanley first crossed the country he found tribes eating their fellow human beings. When they were not eaten, captive members of enemy tribes were sold downriver to white slave traders.

In the upper Congo, black Arabs from East Africa were particularly active in the slave trade at the time of Stanley's expeditions. Stanley records one encounter he had with a group of these raiders in 1883 on the Congo River:

I was permitted in the afternoon to see the human harvest they had gathered. ... The first general impressions are that the camp is much too densely peopled for comfort. There are rows upon rows of dark nakedness ... lines or groups of naked forms upright, standing, or moving about listlessly ... countless naked children, many mere infants ... occasionally a drove of absolutely naked old women bending under a basket of fuel or cassava tubers, or bananas, who are driven through the moving groups by two or three musketeers. ... There is not one adult man-captive among them ...

The slave traders admit they have only 2,300 captives in this fold, yet they have raided through the length and breadth of a country larger than Ireland, bearing fire and spreading carnage with lead and iron. Both banks of the river show that 118 villages and 43 districts have been devastated, out of which is educed this scant profit of 2,300 females and children, and about 2,000 tusks of ivory! The spears, swords, bows, and the quivers of arrows, show that many adults have fallen. Given that these 118 villages were peopled only by 1,000 each, we have only a profit of two per cent; and by the time all these captives have been subjected to the accidents of the river voyage, of camp life and its harsh miseries, to the havoc of smallpox, there will only remain a scant one per cent upon the bloody venture. (*Ibid.*, p. 141)

When King Leopold took over the Congo, the slave trade was outlawed, but another form of exploitation was introduced: forced labor to gather wild rubber. If workers did not produce enough—if their quota was not met—their hands were cut off. Others were lined up in single file one behind another and shot in a group to save bullets. This encouraged the rest to achieve their quota. All profits were immediately sent to Belgium: the purpose of colonization was to enrich the colonizer.

In the later years of the colonial period the Belgians did begin to develop the country for the people. Schools were built, along with hospitals, roads, and railroads. Just prior to independence, the Belgian Congo had one of the highest literacy rates in Africa. But the Belgians did not share the philosophy of the British and the French, who located bright students and helped them to attain higher education. Rather, they promoted a minimum education for the largest number possible; practically no one was permitted to go beyond sixth grade. When independence was forced on the Belgians in 1960, the country could count fewer than a dozen university graduates. Less than 25,000 people had any kind of secondary school training, and the chaos that followed was virtually inevitable. As an independent nation, the people continued to suffer and die in terrible numbers.

It was only after five years of violent turmoil that an army general named Mobutu took power and began to restore stability. He said at the start of his reign that he wanted to make the country into a place the world wouldn't laugh at. He could have added " ... and that people of concern and compassion wouldn't weep over."

Christian missionaries—Catholics from Portugal—had come into the lower Zaire River in the 1400's, but they had penetrated only a few miles into the interior. It was not until the colonial era that missionaries reached the heart of the Congo. Protestant missionaries also started coming into the Belgian Congo in the late 1800's. First came British Baptists, followed by others from Europe and the United States.

The first Disciples missionaries arrived in the country and started work in Equator Region (where we would be going) in 1899. By the early 1970's the membership of the Disciples Community was estimated at over 200,000. All administrative responsibilities were turned over to Zairois leadership in 1957, and since that time missionary personnel have worked under the supervision of local leaders.

In recent years the church had become interested in development work—agricultural projects and other ventures to help the economy. A particular concern had been relating to the staggering needs of the cities.

In colonial days, the Belgians had imposed "Influx Control laws" which severely limited the right of people in the interior to move to towns. Before they could move, they had to present documentation showing that they had a job and wouldn't simply be another unemployed mouth to feed. The Africans hated this law, because they saw the city as synonymous with a better life. The few who got into the towns *did*, in fact, enjoy a higher standard of living than their poorer relatives stuck in the jungle villages.

With independence, the Influx Control laws were struck down immediately, and masses of people began to pour into the towns and cities, only to find a lack of jobs, no housing, and disorder compounded by a chaotic political situation. Since Mobutu had come to power, the political situation had stabilized, but the grinding poverty remained.

The more we read and studied the situation, the more we realized what enormous challenges we were facing. When we permitted ourselves to think of all the problems, we became depressed. What could we do in such a vast sea of overwhelming needs? But we kept digging. After three months of study, we gradually learned to put the discouraging statistics in the back of our minds and to tackle one obstacle at a time.

And now it was time to get back to basics. We couldn't do anything if we couldn't talk to the people, so once again we took up French. Three more months of study, but this time in Paris!

"Taxi! Taxi! Here's one. Hey, can we all get in that little thing?"

"No way," Linda replied. "Hail a second one."

"Taxi! Linda, take Georgia and the luggage in that one. Chris, Kim, and Faith, get in this one with me. *Bonjour, Monsieur. Nous voudrions aller au pension 78 rue d'Assas.*" The driver roared off down the wide avenue leading from Paris' Orly airport, on his way, we hoped, to Number 78 Assas Street. That was where we would stay for the next three months.

Kim looked at me with an astonished smile. "Daddy, I think he understood you!"

"I hope so."

Sure enough, within a few minutes we were pulling up in front of a building with the number 78 on it, and with a street sign on the corner reading "rue d'Assas." I felt positively triumphant.

A *pension* is a boardinghouse catering to people who need a place to stay for a few weeks or months. Arrangements can be made for one, two, or three meals a day, to be eaten in the common dining hall. Our *pension* at 78 rue d'Assas was an old five-story building with a winding, narrow staircase ... and no elevator. By the time we had pushed, pulled, and dragged our luggage up four flights of steps, we were completely exhausted.

"You mean we've gotta climb up and down all those steps for *three months?*" complained Kim.

"That's right."

"Oh, my aching legs!"

"Oh, *our* aching legs," Linda retorted. "All of us are going to share the joy of hauling Georgia up and down these steps!"

Within the coming days we arranged for Chris and Kim to enroll in public school, and we found a kindergarten for Faith and a housewife to keep eighteen-month-old Georgia. Linda and I enrolled in the "Interlangue," a private school specializing in short, intensive courses in French and English.

We attended classes for five hours a day. Each day's program consisted of oral instruction in a class with one professor for each six to ten students; television instruction featuring scenes or short skits which students were required to repeat or interpret; intensive drills in French phrases and sentences, using headphones; and, finally, comprehensive written exercises.

The learning experience was exhausting but exciting too. French was the only common language in classes which included students from Russia, Germany, Japan, Libya, and other countries. Sharing ideas and making friends through the medium of another language was exhilarating. By the end of the course our French wasn't perfect, but we could make ourselves understood. And we were beginning to understand others ... if they didn't talk too fast.

Back at the *pension*, life was not exactly luxurious. The two rooms which the six of us shared were tiny; the food was definitely not of the caliber which has made Paris famous for its cuisine; and we were attacked by bedbugs. When the children and Linda broke out in itching sores and welts, we visited a doctor. After several trips and various kinds of medicines and ointments which did not help, we discovered the bedbugs. The landlady was absolutely outraged.

"That's not possible!" she screamed. "We don't have such little beasts here. You brought them in your luggage from America!"

When we presented the evidence she was genuinely upset, and declared total warfare on the small monsters. Within a few days the enemy was destroyed, our welts disappeared, and life became more pleasant.

A few weeks later our landlady was again shocked when we reported that our room had been broken into while we were eating and that nearly one hundred francs had been stolen.

"It is not possible!" she insisted again. "We don't have thieves in this pension."

But when another room on our floor was robbed the next day, she had to admit there was a thief somewhere on the premises. Again she declared war on the problem, ripping out all the door locks and replacing them with new and stronger ones. In addition, she reimbursed us for the stolen money.

Right across the street from our *pension* were the magnificent Luxembourg Gardens, with rows of stately trees, fountains and pools, statues on shady walks, and play areas for children. If we sensed the blues coming on, we retreated to this beautiful refuge. This always restored our spirits and before long we would feel sufficiently cheerful to return to the fourth floor of our old *pension*, with its bedbugs, thieves, cramped rooms, dingy toilet, and lackluster food.

Week ends in Paris were our adventure and discovery times. On Sunday mornings we usually attended the little Protestant church down the street from our *pension*, and the remaining hours of the day were spent in exploring Paris and its suburbs. The Louvre, with its thousands of priceless works of art, was our favorite destination. At other times we visited the Eiffel Tower and many other famous and not-so-famous landmarks and churches around the city. At Easter we attended a packed service in Notre Dame Cathedral.

In spite of assorted inconveniences, our experience in Paris was a good one. We learned more French, made some fine friends, saw the sights ... and our desire to get to Zaire increased to near fever pitch.

Finally it was June 30, 1973, and tomorrow we would fly. Destination: the Republic of Zaire. We were excited.

4

Mbandaka

AS our family left the plane and approached the terminal building at the Mbandaka airport, there was a sudden feeling of unreality. After all those months of study and preparation, and another long plane ride with four children, were we finally here?

Then, from behind us, a friendly voice greeted us. Bishop Boyaka Inkomo, head of the Disciples Community in Equator Region, had recently returned from the States, where he and his wife had spent six months studying English. What a welcome sound—we had indeed reached our destination.

Mbandaka is the capital city of Equator Region in Zaire. It is situated on the east bank of the wide Zaire River, 412 miles upriver from the national capital Kinshasa. The Ruki River runs into the Zaire River just north of the city, and this area was a trade center long before the white man arrived.

It was Stanley of Stanley and Livingstone fame, however, who put it on the world's maps by locating the Equator Station here. He established the station officially on June 17, 1883, and the first officers in charge were Coquilhat and Vangele. On October 11 of that year, Stanley described an already thriving town in his diary:

Equator Station is certainly a happy one, not so situated with regard to view as it might be; but with that sole exception, many other requisites necessary for well-being are in perfection. We have abundance of food, obtained very cheaply, and the prices are now so established to everyone's content that there is nothing left to complain of. ... Bananas, sweet cassava, potatoes, yams, eggs, Indian corn, poultry, goats, sheep, the native productions assisted by vegetables of Europe flourishing in the gardens, with tea, coffee, sugar, butter, lard, rice, and wheat flour from Europe, afford a sufficient variety for a sumptuous menu. I have enjoyed puddings every day here. ... We have sufficient acreage near the station to be able, if necessary, to feed everybody abundantly ... *

The station grew into a city known as Coquilhatville, until it was renamed Mbandaka in 1971. In October of 1971, Mobutu Sese Seko, president of the Democratic Republic of Congo, inaugurated his name-changing policy as part of his program to bring "authenticity" back to his nation. He changed his own.

The Congo and the Founding of Its Free State, by Henry M. Stanley, Vol. II, page 73.

name (which had been Joseph Désiré Mobutu), the name of the country, the names of major cities, and the names of the citizens. The capital city of Leopoldville became Kinshasa, and the cities of Stanleyville and Elizabethville became Kisangani and Lubumbashi respectively. President Mobutu made it unlawful for any citizen to use his Christian name; only tribal African names could be used.

When we arrived in this same city nearly one hundred years later, it was hard to recognize Stanley's description. What had been a city of 30,000 people as late as 1960 was now jammed with 150,000, most of them living below the "poverty line." Hunger and disease and squalid living conditions were typical, despite the area's rich variety of natural resources.

We began our first Sunday in Mbandaka by visiting one of the thirteen parishes. In the following weeks we visited a different one each Sunday. Always we were welcomed with a hearty handshake. The services were never shorter than two hours, which got to be a bit too much for Georgia. When we stepped outside, we usually found a crowd of children staring at the conspicuous strangers. But our smiles soon turned their stares into smiles, and before long Georgia had twenty or thirty new friends.

These churches treated us like honored guests, which was sometimes a little uncomfortable for us, but seemed to be a pleasure for them. The best chairs would be arranged upfront for us, while the congregation sat on low rough logs or hard benches. And often after we had visited a church, some of the members would come to our home bringing chickens, eggs, pineapples—whatever they had. Most of these gifts, we knew, represented a great sacrifice on their part, and we were reluctant to accept them, but to refuse would have been an unforgivable insult.

Only one of the thirteen parishes had a French service; the rest were in Lingala. Not knowing any Lingala, we didn't always understand the singing and preaching, but we surely could feel the presence of Christ's spirit. Actually, the official language of Zaire is French, but it is used mostly among educated men. Lingala, the river trade language, is the most commonly used of the two hundred languages and dialects spoken in the country, and is the official language of the army. Kikongo, Tshiluba, and Kiswahili are also spoken by many people, and those, along with Lingala, are officially recognized by the government. In Mbandaka, only Lingala and French, of the official languages, are spoken, but there is also a local tribal language called Lonhundo. This is the official tongue of the Disciples Community of Equator Region, and the church people proudly refer to it as "the language of heaven."

The climate in Mbandaka is eternal summertime, although there are supposedly four seasons—two rainy and two dry. Even the dry seasons have some rains, and the river rises tremendously during the rainy seasons, sometimes swelling over the banks but rarely flooding the town. Most of the time temperatures are pleasant, only occasionally becoming uncomfortably hot or chilly. The humidity is perpetually high—with laundry sometimes taking three days to dry.

In September of 1973, two months after our arrival, we put Chris and Kim, then thirteen and ten respectively, on the plane bound for Kinshasa and the American School. We disliked being separated from our two older children, but there was nothing else to do. The Mbandaka schools were badly overcrowded, and we might have taken two places away from local children; in addition, much of the instruction was given in Lingala.

Our oldest daughter Faith, aged six, was allowed to enter the Belgian elementary school, and for two-year-old Georgia we found a nursery school run by a nice Belgian lady. Most of her students were Zairois from the educated families in town. Until we managed to find other transportation, Linda rode Georgia the two miles to and from her classes every day on a bicycle.

With all the children off at school, we were able to get down to business. Linda spent much of her time at the typewriter or running errands, while I began dealing with the problems at the Block and Sand Project. One major hindrance to our effort, I soon discovered, would be the workers' chronically poor health. Practically all the men were weakened to some extent by malaria. Frequently they had intestinal worms, some picked up from unsanitary food preparation or eating with unwashed hands and some taken in through their feet, since everyone went barefoot at home. Their diet consisted mainly of *kwanga* (manioc roots), which contains virtually no food value, and *pondu* (manioc leaves), with occasional fish, chicken, monkey, or goat meat, so they were perpetually malnourished. They drank polluted water from shallow wells; firewood to boil the water was too costly.

Medicines were expensive and sometimes impossible to find; a simple illness often became severe because of the long waiting line at the hospital or a fruitless search for medicine. And even a very small wound was likely to become infected through improper care and develop into a serious health hazard. All these factors contributed to the constant absences due to illness, and frequently even when a man was on the job he was too weak and miserable to work at full capacity.

Linda, of course, had to deal with the same kinds of problems at home. We had been told that early missionaries coming to Africa packed their worldly goods in a coffin, realizing they would not be going back. And even though we had arrived armed with all the latest shots and medicines it was impossible to guard against everything.

When Georgia, then three years old, came down with malaria, we thought at first she had an ordinary intestinal virus, and she went downhill at a frightening rate before we began dosing her with the proper medicine. Two months after that bout, more medical treatment was called for when she passed a live ascaris, the giant intestinal roundworm. This is a common thing for African families, but we found that all our careful indoctrination had not adequately prepared us for that episode.

A month later Georgia developed a big sore under left arm, and we thought it was a kind of boil. But one day when she was at the construction site with me, one of the workmen saw it and said it was a worm. He sent one of the men into the forest for a certain kind of leaf. When the man returned with a handful of the leaves, they asked me to lay Georgia on her side. Then they squeezed the juice from the leaves onto the sore. Within ten seconds the lump began to wriggle; half a minute later a hole opened in the center. Then one of the men reached down and popped out a big fat worm. It was incredible. Within a few days the area had healed—and we had reluctantly learned how to deal with another tropical invader.

We saw so many people die for senseless reasons. Digging crews at the cemetery continuously worked overtime. During much of our time in Mbandaka, children were dying all over the area from an epidemic of old-fashioned red measles. Three of Georgia's little neighbor friends, all from the same family, caught the measles and just barely pulled through. Georgia had prayed faithfully for them, and it must have been a gift of grace which saved them, for most did not make it.

Another constant challenge for Linda was to keep supplied with food a household that varied from five to a dozen people. There were several open-air markets throughout the city, with the largest one within walking distance of our house. Lokesa, our *cuisinier*, went there nearly every morning to buy for our kitchen, but we went only occasionally, because the price went up if a white person appeared.

The markets offered a wide variety of indigenous foods such as bananas, plantain (a large tropical fruit similar to the banana), sweet potatoes, manioc, *pili pili* (hot peppers), onions, pineapples, oranges, and avocados. There were all kinds of fish, both smoked and fresh, and local delicacies like antelope liver. This is the tenderest of meats, and we bought it every chance we got. Nothing, however, was weighed or accurately measured. Large items like pineapples, a bag of charcoal, or a bunch of bananas were sold by the piece. Small items such as potatoes, onions, and tomatoes were sold by the pile. Very small or ground foods like peanuts, flour, sugar, and salt were sold by the glass or cupful.

The unavailability of certain food supplies at the most unexpected times made Linda an expert in improvising. She tried, whenever possible, to get staples in bulk, and bought flour and sugar in hundred-pound sacks. Margarine and milk powder came in cans (fresh milk was unavailable). There was one nice meat store in town where we could usually find cuts of beef and pork as well as rounds of imported cheese. But the bakeries were discouragingly dirty—if we could buy bread right out of the oven we could be fairly sure that it was sanitary, but the loaves were never wrapped. If we did not get it fresh from the oven, it was likely to be sold out. Linda baked a lot of our bread and rolls, and fresh pineapple pies—and no one complained much about shortages.

Gardens do well in Mbandaka since there is a continual growing season. We were able to grow many of our fresh vegetables, including spinach, tomatoes, cucumbers, okra, and green beans twelve inches long. By making our own catsup, syrup, yogurt, and powdered milk ice cream, we ate well. I think we really missed only two things: pecans and strawberries.

Sunday was the biggest market day. People came to do their shopping and their socializing. Chickens and goats were tied up everywhere, waiting for a buyer. Bargaining was the order of the day, and a deal was usually terminated with a *"matabish"*—a small bonus given by the seller.

People came to the market on foot with loads of goods on their backs and balanced on their heads; on bicycles with wares piled on and tied by any means possible; and on the trucks which transported both people and goods, loaded down to the axle-breaking point. There simply were not enough transportation facilities. The few old buses that were still running carried more than their limit of passengers. A shortage of capable mechanics added to the problem, and replacement parts were frequently nonexistent.

Driving is dangerous in Mbandaka, not because there are too many cars (actually, there are very few), but because the roads are often filled with hundreds of pedestrians. There are no sidewalks anywhere in the city. The police (gendarmes) advise drivers to keep going and find the nearest gendarme station if they should hit someone on the road. Many people, especially the "old mamas," still believe that if a car injures someone the driver is possessed by an evil spirit and must be killed. If the driver stopped and tried to help someone he hit, a crowd would descend on him and literally beat him to death.

While we were in Mbandaka, the Peace Corps director hit and killed a little girl near our house. She darted in front of his Land Rover, and there was no way he could avoid hitting her. He hurried on to the nearest gendarme station, where he was kept overnight for his own protection. The following day he was allowed to go home, but only in the company of gendarmes, who stayed outside his house constantly for two days. Then a representative of the American Embassy in Kinshasa arrived, and it was decided he should be transferred to another city. It would have been too risky to leave him in Mbandaka.

Often, however, the gendarmes were more nuisance than help. The first month we were there we were arrested no less than twenty times. Finally we realized that it was because we were new white folks in town and they just wanted to get to know us. There are not many road signs and there are no traffic signals, so usually we would commit some traffic violation unawares.

Once Linda made the mistake of stopping her motorbike at an intersection and was whistled down.

"Why did you stop?" inquired the gendarme.

"Because I wanted to see if any cars were coming."

"But you had the right-of-way!"

"I did? Oh, I didn't know. There is no road sign."

"You should know. You committed an infraction. Let's go to the station."

She pleaded with him, explaining she was new in town and did not know who had the right-of-way at that intersection. But he would not be persuaded. Then she pointed out that if they went to the station she would have to ride him on the back of the motorbike, and that she had never ridden anyone before. That didn't scare him. He was determined to take her in!

As they rode through town, startled eyes followed them—a helmeted black soldier riding on the rear of a white woman's unsteady motorbike. As in all the other cases, the officer in charge at the station did not charge Linda a fine. After a somewhat friendly conversation, she was dismissed.

My first encounter with the gendarmes was equally ludicrous.

We had only been in Zaire a couple of weeks. I had ridden into town on the motorbike to check for mail at the post office. On the way back I gave a signal at the first corner and started to turn right. The white-helmeted soldier standing there blew his whistle and started waving his hands and running toward me. I pulled over to the curb.

Hands on hips, he confronted me sternly. "What are you doing?"

"What am I doing? I'm riding my motorbike, and I just turned right!"

"No, what were you doing when you stuck your hand up in the air?" He lifted his left hand high to illustrate his question.

"I was giving the signal to turn right."

"That's not the signal to turn right."

"What do you mean? That is the international signal to turn right."

"But, monsieur, you are in Zaire! Here is the signal for turning right." He extended his right hand straight out, parallel to the ground.

"That's the signal for turning right here?"

"Yes."

"But what if one is in a car? How can you reach over to stick your arm out the window?"

"If you are in a car, you should use the turn signal."

"But what if there isn't a turn signal, and there isn't anyone sitting on the right side to stick his arm out?"

"That would never happen."

Not wanting to argue that point, I pleaded ignorance, saying that we were new in the country, and I asked him to forgive me. I promised to use the Zaire signal for turning right in the future. He let me go.

It was never really clear whether the gendarmes were regular army recruits, but they wore the standard olive green army uniforms, adding a distinctive white helmet with a red band. On many days there were none in town. On others, they were everywhere, with three or four standing together on each corner. On some days they stopped no one; on other days they stopped nearly everybody. They had no vehicles, so they resorted to shrill whistles, arm waving, and running after offenders. If a person failed to stop, the gendarmes could do nothing unless they could commandeer a passing taxi.

Speeding was not an offense. I never heard of anyone who was stopped for going too fast. And parking vehicles in the middle of the street didn't seem to bother the gendarmes. But stopping at an intersection when one had the right-of-way was considered a grave error, as Linda discovered—even though there were practically no signs anywhere indicating who had the right-of-way.

Hesitating a little too long or not hesitating enough before turning at an intersection was another serious offense. Frequently we were stopped for no traffic violation at all; the gendarmes simply wanted to see our identification documents and driving permits, or ask why we were in that part of town. Some days, particularly at the beginning of our stay, I was arrested two and three times. The soldiers sometimes did routine checks of vehicles, and on those days it was nearly impossible to drive around town. Apparently the officials gave all the gendarmes the same instructions. There were no checkpoints—every point was a checkpoint. This meant that you were likely to be stopped at each corner and asked precisely the same question.

In the beginning, being arrested was a bit frightening, but we soon learned what to expect, and fear gave way to annoyance and frustration. And sometimes, in spite of the exasperation of these arrests, they turned out to be very warm human experiences.

One day in 1976 I was in our little Volkswagen, heading for the post office. As I crossed the last intersection, I heard the shrill whistle of a gendarme. Sure enough, another long and irritating discussion with two gendarmes began, finally ending as one left in a huff with my driving permit. I decided to not even try to retrieve it and to ignore the whole episode, something I did frequently toward the end of our time in Zaire.

Three days later, I was down by the river in the early evening, where our crew was unloading sand from the barges. The gendarme appeared who had remained at the corner on the day of my arrest. At first I didn't recognize him, for he was dressed in civilian clothes. As he began to talk, however, I suddenly realized who he was. He told me he had come with my driver's permit.

I felt a flash of anger. I was familiar with this procedure: a license or some other important document would be taken during the daytime, and the arresting officer would come at night to return it, expecting some reward for his service.

"Listen," I said, "if you've come here for money, you can leave. As far as I'm concerned, you can keep the permit. I'm not giving you anything."

"No, no," he objected. "I am not here for money. I am a Christian, and I have been bothered about the way we separated that day. You were angry, and I know you did not feel good toward me. I've come to return your permit and to heal our broken relationship."

Smiling broadly, he handed me the permit and extended his hand. I was speechless.

I invited him into the house. We visited for perhaps an hour, and I saw that the man was really motivated to come by his Christian faith. I was humbled by his action, and ashamed as I recalled my brusque manner toward him three days earlier. I apologized for my rudeness and asked him to extend my apologies to the other gendarme. Reconciliation between us was complete, and we parted good friends.

Our encounters with the gendarmes, as well as with others, were always learning experiences about attitudes and relationships among the Zairois. For example, we found it not uncommon for two men to walk down the road holding hands. This is a sign of close friendship and without the sexual connotations of Western cultures. On the other hand, it is rare to see a boy and girl or husband and wife holding hands or displaying any outward signs of affection in public. The husband almost always goes first, and the wife and children are expected to follow.

There are strong loyalties among people from the same region, village, and extended family. We gradually learned that *"mon petit frère* (my little brother)" did not necessarily mean any blood kinship.

The plight of women is dismal. Of course, it is less so among the educated class, but the woman is generally regarded simply as one who bears children and prepares food (although, interestingly enough, men often do their own personal laundry). The pressures are terrific on the young girls who continue their education beyond sixth grade and thus do not conform to their stereotyped role in society.

If a woman has been unsuccessful in having children, she is likely to be sent back to her village and replaced by one who can produce. Having a limitless number of children gravely endangers the health of the mothers, but in a poverty-stricken culture a man has all his wealth in his children. They are his pride, his helpers, and his security for later years.

True friendships between Zairois and foreigners are difficult. Even if one can communicate well and share in the way of life, there are still stresses and strains. The Zairois think that foreigners have everything and can do anything. There is no end to their demands for favors and requests for money and items such as watches, cameras, and cooking utensils. This becomes a real problem, even though it is understandable from people who are lacking so many things.

Many don't even ask—they just take. Stealing is rampant in Zaire, especially in the cities. Every business establishment and any building with anything of value in it must be guarded at night to prevent theft. The men who guard these places are called *sentinelles*. These scantily-clad protectors of property are usually armed with spears, machetes, and bows and arrows. In Kinshasa, the capital, being a *sentinelle* is a dangerous occupation, for thieves are often armed and prone to violence if accosted during a heist. In Mbandaka robbers are a bit more polite. If they are discovered during a break-in, they simply do their best to get away.

We had three *sentinelles*. One was at the housing project to guard the building supplies; one was at the Block and Sand Project to watch over the block-making equipment, truck, and blocks; the third guarded our house and the boat, barges, and conveyor belt at the unloading dock adjacent to the house.

When we first came to Zaire, I resisted the idea of having someone guard our home. I did not want to live a secluded life, protected from the people we had come to serve. Almost without exception the foreigners in town, including missionaries, had one or more *sentinelles*, plus iron bars over the windows and, in many cases, high concrete walls around the house with broken glass embedded in the top.

In the house assigned to us there were no bars on the windows or walls enclosing the yard, but an earlier missionary had electrically wired the windows and doors to give any intruder an unhealthy shock. The system was not functioning when we moved in and I did not want to reactivate it. We would live in an open house without all this prison paraphernalia separating us from people.

Everything went all right for a few weeks. Then I awoke one night to find a thief cutting down the living-room curtains with a razor blade. He and his cohorts had already stolen food, clothing, camera, dishes, tape recorder, and radio. At that point we decided it was necessary to hire a *sentinelle* for the house and one for the boat and barges because things were being stolen there, too. We still resisted the high walls and the bars over the windows. And in spite of other thefts and attempted thefts throughout our stay, we continued to live in an unprotected house, except for the *sentinelle* at night.

One night soon after we acquired our *sentinelle*, Linda was awakened by a loud ripping noise.

"What was that?" she yelled, sitting up abruptly.

My eyes snapped open. There was a thief right beside our bed tearing open the screen in order to come into the house. When he heard Linda, he took off.

The *sentinelle* was fast asleep on the other side of the house. A few nights later, when I found him asleep again, I gently stole the shoes off his feet. The next morning I gave them back and fired him.

The second *sentinelle* was a lot more conscientious, but there were thefts and attempted thefts even after he came. Once two thieves were trying to pry open the front door, and the *sentinelle*, hiding in the shrubbery, jumped up and threw his spear at them. They dropped the big screwdriver they were using to jimmy the lock and high-tailed it down the road.

This episode prompted the *sentinelle* to ask if he would be put in prison if he killed a thief trying to break into the house.

"No," I said, "but I don't want you killing anyone. If it comes to the point of having to kill to prevent a theft, let the robbers have what they want. Even a thief is a human being, and we should not try to take his life, which is more precious than any amount of things."

He didn't agree with me. He thought it much more sensible to kill the man, if possible. So I strongly admonished him not to kill under any circumstances. Our *sentinelles* were instructed to use whatever measures seemed necessary to prevent a theft up to the point of taking someone's life; but if a situation came to that they were to let the culprits go.

Rarely did a week pass that something was not stolen. At the housing project we would place stakes in the ground laying off a new house and return the following morning to find them stolen. Once a man in town hired some boys to steal planks from the project. He paid them five makutas (five cents) a plank, and sold the planks for two dollars each! Small items, especially, were stolen consistently—hammers, buckets, shovels, machetes. Every few weeks we would have to buy a new supply of these tools. When Larry Stoner found a really deluxe wheelbarrow in Kinshasa, he bought it for the project and brought it upriver on the boat. We were able to use it two weeks before it disappeared.

At the Block and Sand Project, tire tools, jacks and wrenches were constantly "walking off." Periodically, the steel cable used on the crane would be stolen; it was valuable to local people for making animal traps. We also used this steel cable to tie the boat to the connected sand barges, pushing them between the anchored barge and the unloading dock on the shore.

Late one afternoon, just before dark, the *sentinelle* came running to my door yelling that the boat was floating down the river. I raced out with him to discover that a thief had come along in a dugout canoe and had stolen both the cables that connected the boat to the sand barges. On several previous occasions thieves had stolen one of the cables, but they had always been polite enough to leave the other, so that the boat would remain connected to the barges. This time the rogue had taken both cables and let the boat drift off down the river.

I had to hunt for the boat captain and then locate an outboard motor and dugout canoe to chase the boat. By the time all this was done, the boat was several miles downstream. We finally caught up with it and chugged our way back home, arriving after midnight.

On four different occasions our boat was broken into and tools, batteries, and other items were stolen. Once the thieves tried to dismount the entire motor, but they couldn't get some of the nuts off the bolts. Most of the thefts occurred at night, but the boat was robbed once at noon on Sunday, while we were sitting only a short distance away eating lunch!

One evening we were having supper when the lights suddenly went out down on the shore where we unloaded sand. I hurried out only to discover a thief running up the road with the meter box. He had cut the live 220-volt electric line with a machete and ripped the box off the wall with his bare hands!

My favorite means of transportation in Mbandaka was my little blue motorbike. When I was in town one afternoon, I went into a store for a couple of minutes, and during that brief interval two boys ran off with the bike. I thought I would never see it again, but two weeks later I was driving in the outskirts of Mbandaka, and saw the motorbike in front of a little house. I stopped my car and walked over, to discover it was a gendarme station. I asked to speak to the chief.

When I told him he had my motorbike, the chief smiled and said, "Yes, I'm sure we do. I remember seeing you riding it around town. We got it from a boy a couple of days ago when we were stopping people on routine checks of ownership documents. You may take it."

For once I was pleased that the gendarmes were diligent in asking people for their papers!

When we had first arrived in Mbandaka, and saw the house in which we were to live, the possibility that our belongings might be stolen could not have been farther from our minds. The initial sight that greeted us was two men shoveling manure out of the bathtub. It seemed the church had allowed an American family to live in the house who believed in a "back to nature" life-style, to the extent that goats, chickens, and monkeys were allowed to roam freely indoors. Outside, a lovely fountain and wading pool in the yard was so overgrown and filled with trash that many days elapsed before we even discovered its existence. Linda lay awake several nights figuring ways to deodorize the place, and it took a crew of six workmen from the church, plus our family, two weeks to clear all sorts of debris, scrub and paint before we could move in. We found it strange that the church had known we were coming for months, but waited until the day of our arrival to begin preparing our lodging. However, other missionaries assured us this was nothing out of the ordinary.

When the house was finally made livable, it became a joy to us throughout our three-year stay. Originally built by the

Belgian businessman who had also established the Block and Sand Project, it was a rambling two-story structure with a beautiful view of the Zaire River only a few yards away. When the truck was broken down or the conveyor belt wouldn't run or the electricity conked out, we still had those lovely evenings along the water.

We also got to know the big riverboats and barges that passed from time to time. Someone would shout, "Here comes the I.T.B. from Kinshasa!" or "Here comes the Kinshasa-Boende boat!" Everyone watched closely, because the pirogues (dugouts) would often upset as they worked their way over to tie up to the big boat. Many people made their livelihood selling to the passengers, and it was an art to maneuver within grabbing distance of the side and hold on while selling fish, bunches of plantains, ivory objects, baskets, pottery, and other crafts.

Once when we were on the boat from Kinshasa to Mbandaka, we saw a pirogue overturn, spilling out two men and several cases of beer. So far as we knew, the men drowned. Our boat was going too fast to stop and help, and the distance was too great for them to swim ashore.

Our children studied the cargo boats and freight barges traveling the river with shipments of Land Rovers, trucks, cars, and machinery just as children in the States count the cars in a freight train. Also, there was a big wood market just down the beach from us, and everyone watched the constant parade of pirogues loaded with lumber from the forest, with manioc, and with clay pots. A few of these dugouts had been motorized with outboards, but generally they were powered by men and women using long-handled paddles. The most exciting river spectacle of all occurred whenever President Mobutu's huge and powerful boat went by, raising high waves and crashing pirogues along the shore.

Another family pleasure was taking a picnic to the former Botanical Gardens a few miles north of the city. Originally said to have had one of the most complete collections of flora in the world, these gardens were a major tourist attraction during the Belgian administration. Now the lack of interest along with insufficient funds had allowed them to deteriorate. They were still a refuge of delight for us, however, just as the Luxembourg Gardens had been in Paris.

Tropical bugs and diseases; lengthy family separations; difficult culture adjustments; struggles with unfamiliar languages. These and many other problems were with us throughout our years in Mbandaka. But it was a city of great opportunities and fascinating people, and we thanked God for the rich experience of serving Him there.

5

The Block and
Sand Project

OUR principal assignment in Zaire was to aid the church in
Equator Region with its development projects. At the time of
our arrival, there were about a dozen such projects, ranging
from a coffee plantation to a small hotel. The church requested
that I study all these enterprises and make suggestions concerning what should be done with each of them.

There were three agricultural projects. One project, some
twenty miles south of Mbandaka, had been raising bananas,
peanuts and corn. A year or so earlier a Peace Corps volunteer
had worked with the project, but when he left the Zairois
director either was not capable or was not sufficiently interested to keep the venture going. When I visited the site, the
weeds reigned supreme. It was difficult even to find the path
leading into the project. Three workmen and the director were
sitting on the ground, idly chatting. Obviously nothing had
been produced there for months.

The second project was at Bolenge, about five miles south of
Mbandaka. This had been a big enterprise, headed for several
years by a Disciples missionary. They had several hundred
laying hens, as well as geese, ducks, rabbits, beef cattle, and
many kinds of vegetables. A year prior to our arrival,
however, the missionary had fallen gravely ill and had had to
abandon the effort. Local leadership took over and the project
went downhill. All the rabbits were stolen. Most of the chickens were stolen or had died. All gardening had ceased. The
only stock that remained was thirty head of cattle ... along
with the Zairois director and ten workers! Each worker had
about two chickens to take care of, while one man tended the
cattle. Not too much going on there, either.

In addition to the agricultural project at Bolenge, there
were two other enterprises in that village. One was a garage.
When we visited it, we were told all the tools had been stolen
and the business had not been able to operate for over a year.

The other project was a theater. A former church building
had been converted into a place to show films. The church had
purchased a projector in the United States and had secured

some films, but the projector had burned up the first night it was used. No one had been able to get it to work after that.

The third agricultural project was a coffee plantation located at Lokole, a village some four hundred miles east of Mbandaka. Without a vehicle suitable for such a long trip, we couldn't visit this project at first. A year later, when we were able to travel to Lokole, we found the plantation completely overgrown with weeds and producing virtually nothing.

Another project was a bookstore. When we arrived there its display room stood practically empty, with a couple of young women lounging behind the counter. There were no customers. The storage room in the back, however, was packed with all kinds of books—Bibles, hymnals, storybooks—almost all of which were covered with mold. Some were so badly damaged by the dampness that they were unusable. The director of this bookstore was also the director of a related project—a print shop. When I talked with him, he complained that he had no money to buy paper, and that's why the print shop wasn't working. He also said he didn't have funds for materials to sell in the bookstore. When I asked him why he didn't display the books he already had, he mumbled something about needing to get them out.

The small-hotel project—known as the "Guest House"—had been occupied by missionaries when we had visited Mbandaka in 1966, and there was an apartment reserved for visitors in which we had lived during our stay. At that time the place was immaculately clean, with flowers planted all over the spacious yard. When we arrived this time the building had a small restaurant, two apartments, and several rooms to rent out on a daily basis. The flowers were gone, and two septic tanks were overflowing into the yard, giving the area a terrible odor. The rooms were in total disrepair and hadn't been painted in years. We hardly recognized the building as the same place at which we had stayed seven years earlier.

In Mbandaka the Block and Sand Project was producing—like all the other ventures—nothing. But I could see some hope for it. What's more, I had to get it going again if we were to realize our dream of a housing development. The operation consisted of two block-making machines; a dump truck; three barges; a crane (mounted in the middle of the Zaire River to dig sand from the river bottom); a tugboat (to push the sand barges back and forth between the crane and the shore; a conveyor belt (to unload the sand from the barges onto the dump truck); a work shed under which the blocks were made; and a long building which contained the office, tool shop, and cement storage room. The project had a director and fourteen workmen. At the time of our arrival in 1973, no sand had been taken from the river for two months and no blocks had been produced. The workers had received no salary for the past month.

The conveyor belt had fallen into the river some months earlier, bending it into an arch shape, but the men had managed to pull it out and get it running again after a fashion. The belt itself was a patchwork of leather, wire, cloth, cord, and rubber. All bearings on the machine were completely worn out. The wooden planks on which the concrete blocks were made had almost all been eaten by termites, so only a few blocks could be made each day. Only one of the two block-making machines was in running condition; the second one had been gutted in an attempt to keep the first one going. The barges were full of holes that had been "patched" by pouring tons of cement in the bottom. They were barely afloat and everyone expected them to sink any day. The truck was old— it was the one we had helped purchase after our 1966 trip. The tires were worn out. The electric generator acquired for the project five years earlier had been wired improperly, and on its very first day in use a part had burned up; it had sat there ever since. (There is city electricity in Mbandaka but the current is cut off frequently, and if one doesn't have an alternate source of power, many hours—and sometimes days—can be wasted.) As a final disaster, there was no cement ... and no money with which to buy any!

After visiting these projects and studying them over a period of weeks, I was sorely depressed. Where could I start in such a sea of failures? Pastor Boyaka and I discussed the question at great length, and finally concluded that I should give priority attention to the Block and Sand Project, with the goal of putting it back into good running order and then launching a housing program.

For the other projects, I would serve as an adviser to the existing directors and would try to help them put their respective ventures into functioning condition. (In this second assignment, I was an almost total failure. I did not have time to personally supervise the work in these widely scattered places, and my advice just didn't take. Over the next few months all the other projects, except the "Guest House" and the print shop, closed down.)

The Block and Sand Project was important not only for the proposed housing scheme but also because it was the only enterprise of its kind in the city. (In fact, there was just one other "industry" in the city—a beer factory employing about two hundred people.) The Project was the only source of commercially made concrete blocks, and it had the only equipment for scooping sand from the river bottom. Thus the development of all of Mbandaka would suffer if this venture collapsed.

The church had obtained the Project in the first place because of its economic importance to the city. The operation had been started by a Belgian businessman who had fled the country at independence. He returned five years later with the intention of dismantling the business and shipping the equipment downriver to Kinshasa to be sold. But the local government authorities did not want the city to lose this enterprise. They approached church leaders and pleaded with them to buy the business and operate it for the benefit of the people, admitting they had neither the money nor the personnel to maintain the venture.

Local church leaders contacted the Disciples missionary office in Indianapolis and presented their case for buying the Project. Together they decided it would be a wise investment. The church needed blocks and sand for its own new buildings, and the Project would also have the potential for producing sorely needed income, while at the same time it would serve a vital function for the general population. Purchase arrangements were quickly made with the owner, and soon the church was in the block-making business.

Over the years, the Project served the church well, providing materials for the new administrative building, several new churches, and a dormitory for the Protestant Girls' School, while at the same time selling sand and blocks to the public. By the time of our arrival, however, the business was all but dead. It would be a gigantic task to get it to functioning properly again.

Our greatest need was money. I began my search with a letter to my friend, Dr. David Stowe, Executive Vice President of the United Church Board for World Ministries (United Church of Christ). This board had already officially recognized our ministry in Zaire with the designation of "associated service status," so I felt they would be receptive to a plea for funds.

On August 7, 1973, I wrote the following letter:

We need money! My priority task is to get this Block and Sand operation going. By doing so we can precipitate other things—like the house-building scheme. And I need to move quickly because my tour of service will be up all too soon. Out here it takes four times as long to do almost anything.

I've been here for over a month, and even though we've got fourteen men on the payroll at the Block and Sand Project, not one block has been produced. There are multiple reasons for this and money will not solve all the problems—work attitudes must be changed for one thing—but money will greatly help at this point because it will enable us to replace this junk we are trying to work with.

For example, look at the enclosed photo of the conveyor belt that is used in unloading the sand from the barges onto the dump truck. This thing was an old piece of equipment when the church bought it years ago. You can imagine how it runs now! It takes three days of repairs to operate it half a day. And everything else is equally ancient; the block-making machines, the crane, the barges, etc.

I don't have exact cost figures yet on replacing and repairing everything, but I think it will be somewhere around ten to fifteen thousand dollars. I wonder if the Board could give us a grant of say five thousand dollars to kick this thing off? That much would enable us to move quickly to replace and repair the really bad things, and get us started again. Then I'd have time to get the other needed funds while we are operating.

I will continue to keep you posted as I move into other areas of the work. I think at this point that I am going to advise the church to close down most of the projects. They are terribly mismanaged, and probably the church should never have gotten into much of this stuff in the first place ...

Early in September the grant was made. We were on our way to getting back into business! In the meantime, we struggled along with the old junk. The daily frustrations of running the project often fell into the "unbelievable" category. I wrote the following letter to Bob Nelson, Africa Secretary for the Disciples, about my experiences on one of my workdays—and believe me, the day was not untypical!

October 3, 1973

Dear Bob:

I thought you might like to know how our life is going here, so here's one recent day, blow by blow:

Normally, my day starts at 7 A.M. with the fourteen men who work in the Block and Sand Project, out under the big palm trees for a time of hymn singing, sharing of our faith, and prayer. Then we fan out to our work to make blocks, haul sand, etc.

But on this Wednesday morning at seven o'clock it was raining like crazy (we're in the rainy season now), so only four of the men were at the work site. We stood around under the work shed for twenty minutes or so, and the rain just kept coming in ever-increasing force. We decided to skip our worship time. You couldn't hear, anyway, under that tin roof.

I told the four men to start turning on end the blocks we'd made the day before, in order to remove the wooden pallets that each block is placed on when it is made. By 8 A.M. this operation was completed. The rain had slackened a bit, and some of the other men were beginning to drift in. I told them to get the machine ready to make blocks. By 8:30 A.M. the machine was set up and we started production.

The rain had now practically stopped, so I went down to the river (about 500 yards away) with half a dozen men to unload sand from the barges onto the dump truck. But before we had loaded one truckload, one of the workmen came with word that the block-making machine had broken down. I rushed back to see about it.

I hadn't been there ten minutes when one of the men from the river detail ran up to tell me that the conveyor belt, which transports the sand from the barges to the truck, was broken. By this time, we had discovered that the oil had leaked out of the block-making machine, so I sent a man to buy some more. Then I started in a trot back toward the river.

A young man about seventeen years old stopped me on the way. He had come to inquire about the pay due his father, who had been working for the Block and Sand Project until his death last month. The policy of the church is to continue full pay for three months after the death of an employee. This boy's family had not received anything this month, however, because the income from the Block and Sand Project had not been sufficient even to pay all the living workers. Amid his urgent and repeated assertions that he and his family were hungry—which I'm sure they were—I explained regretfully that there was no money now, but that we were finally making blocks and selling sand, and I *hoped* that by Friday we'd have enough money to pay him. He trudged off with a long face and I resumed my trot to the river.

The belt was badly broken, and I knew it would take hours to repair it. You wouldn't believe the condition this belt is in—really it is a comic strip of leather, cord, wire, cloth, and rubber. So I told the boat captain to get the boat, attach it to the barges, and pull them downstream a bit, to a place where we could throw the sand from the barges directly onto the truck. While he was doing this, I had the men use their shovels to fill the truck, digging up the sand around the conveyor belt. I urgently wanted to get *something* accomplished, because by this time it was midmorning and we hadn't produced a thing.

Shoveling the sand was slow going, but finally the truck was full, and I sent the driver to deliver it to one of our customers. While he was gone, we prepared the driveway down to the new loading site. Just as we were finishing this job, the truck driver came up in a taxi to tell me that the truck was stuck in the mud, and I had to send three men to help him get it out.

By this time it was nearly noon, so I went back up to the block-making site to see how they were coming along. After three hours, they had just gotten the machine back together, with new oil in it, only to discover that the merchant had sold them an inferior grade of oil that wouldn't work in that motor. So they had to start taking it apart again to clean out all the bad oil; then they would get oil of the right kind. I dragged myself home to eat a bit of lunch.

My first task after lunch was to help load the sand from the new site. The truck was out of the mud by this time, and I thought that at last we were set for a productive afternoon of work. I had the driver back the truck down the new road and then go out again, because I wanted to make sure the road was solid enough. He had no trouble, so I decided we could load up. We started throwing the sand directly from the barges onto the truck with shovels. This was painfully slow, but better than sitting and doing nothing.

Suddenly, a young boy ran up to announce excitedly that his mother had just been arrested by the military at the market. The boy's father was one of our workers, so I told him to go with his son and see what the trouble was.

We continued to load the sand. Finally the truck was full. The driver was to deliver the load to an instructor at one of our mission schools. He started the truck up the road and it promptly sank down—to the axles.

I wallowed around in the mud until 2:30, trying to get the truck out, without any success. Then I went to the other work site and found the men still trying to clean out the bad oil. I told them to continue with this, but that I would have to leave because I had five one-legged men sitting at my house, waiting for me to take them to the missionary clinic at Bolenge to be measured for new wooden legs.

I now walked half a mile to the home of Bob Williams, another missionary, to borrow his Volkswagen bus, and by a little after three o'clock we were on the road, bouncing from one mud hole to the next. I kept hoping we wouldn't get *that* vehicle stuck in the mud ...

Seven days later I wrote a letter to another friend, Bob Wood of Westport, Connecticut, describing yet another day of my experiences in the Block and Sand Project.

October 10, 1973

Dear Bob,

The Block and Sand Project continues to make slow progress. I've *got* to get it in good working order as a precondition to starting the housing project. But that's not easy! Just let me tell you about yesterday, and I think you'll begin to understand some of the difficulties associated with this task.

My day started early, as usual—about 6 A.M. After breakfast with the family, I rode into town with little Georgia on my motorbike, to take her to nursery school. On the way in I got arrested by the military (no police here, only soldiers—lots of them, too). They charged me with holding Georgia improperly on the scooter and not having proper papers. Probably nothing will come of this. I've been arrested before, but it's usually just a nuisance.

When I returned to my house a couple of my one-legged friends were here to be taken to the clinic at Bolenge to be measured for legs. I had to tell them to come back next week, because we're out of the forms from the hospital at Kimpese.

Just then Pastor Bolongwa, work foreman at the Block and Sand Project, came rushing up to the house to say that something was wrong with the boat that pushes the sand barges. He said it was in the middle of the river, just floating by, and the men on board were waving their arms around. I ran out to the river bank, and, sure enough, there was our boat, slowly drifting down toward Kinshasa. (That's almost 500 miles, but I immediately had visions of its going all the way before we could stop it!)

We ran up the shore and got in a dugout canoe that had a small motor and putt-putted out to the boat. The men told us they had gone out to the crane, which is mounted in the river, disconnected the boat from the barges, and started back to shore with a Portuguese man I had sent out this morning to give me an estimate on repairing our barges, when the drive shaft had broken. There was no way to make it go again.

I told them to hang on and we'd try to find another boat to pull them to shore. I asked the Portuguese fellow if he could pull us with his boat.

"No," he replied; "it is broken down."

A quarter of a mile down the shore from us a Belgian businessman has a boat repair shop with many boats parked along the water's edge. I zipped in there just knowing I'd get a boat right away. But the foreman told me all the boats were "*en panne* (broken down)."

"You mean to tell me that *all* the boats are broken down!" I said.

"Yes, every one."

I insisted, "*Every one?*"

"Well," he said, "there is one that belongs to one of our customers. I think it might run after some minor repairs."

"Then let's fix it up and go. My boat is on its way to Kinshasa. This is an emergency!"

"Can't go now," he replied, "I must have authorization from another man who isn't here."

"Where is he?" I asked.

"Don't know. You'll just have to wait."

I didn't know where any more boats were, so I sat there and watched my boat drift out of sight down the river.

Then the other man arrived. I ran up to him with an air of great urgency, trying to create some excitement and interest in getting the boat *quickly*. I explained the situation, and he calmly replied that I'd have to get permission from someone else—the owner of the shop.

"Where is he?"

"Don't know."

Thoroughly frustrated, I started running up the path to our house to get my motorbike and start a search when the owner of the shop drove in. I raced back and explained the situation all over again. Thank goodness! He was decisive. He ordered the men to get the boat ready as soon as possible, and go after our boat.

After five minutes he left, and the men began absolutely creeping around getting the boat ready, with no urgency at all. First, they screwed on a little piece of pipe. Then they brought down a battery and slowly connected it up. Then they tried the motor and found that the battery was dead. They strolled up to get another one. This time the motor started. We pushed the boat out into the river, but when the captain put it in gear nothing happened.

For once they got in a hurry, fell to their knees and peered over the back of the boat, and discovered that the propeller was gone. We all frantically grabbed for the tail end of one of the other boats before we ended up having another boat drifting down the river.

As soon as we had pulled the big boat back to shore the creeping started again. The men went off looking for the propeller; I waited about twenty minutes and then went looking for them.

I found my repair man sitting in front of the shop having a snack. I almost lost my "Christian cool."

"Where is the propeller?" I demanded to know.

"Oh," he replied, "I found it, but the bolt that holds it on is missing."

"Well," I said, "get another one."

"There's *not* another one."

"What are you going to do?"

"I don't know."

Just then, we heard a boat come in out front. I asked the man if we could possibly borrow that boat.

"We'll ask," he said.

We marched out to the new people, and my man started this long discussion in Lingala which I thought would never end. Finally, he gave me the news. They would go and get my boat, but they wanted to charge me a fee directly without giving the garage a commission. The man couldn't authorize this without the owner's permission.

Once again: "Where is he?"

"Don't know! Maybe at his house. Maybe in town."

I got on my trusty motorbike and raced all over town for perhaps thirty minutes looking for the owner. No luck.

I returned to the garage. The repair man said maybe the owner was out toward Bolenge at his father's house. I asked him to jump on the motorbike and show me the way. We bounced to the father's house—about four miles away—and found him there.

My man explained the situation to his boss and the reply was, "No. We must have our commission. He can't go out from our place and charge a fee without giving us a cut."

So the old money business stopped that hopeful possibility. The greed of the two men kept either one from getting a fee, and it kept me from getting the boat.

I asked the owner if he knew of any other boat I might get. He said No, but maybe I could get one at Secli-Wenzi, a village about fifteen miles downriver. He figured the missing boat was about there by this time—it was now 1 P.M.!

"But," I said, "I don't have enough fuel in my scooter to get down there and back. Is there a service station between here and there?"

"No. You must return to Mbandaka, get your fuel, and then come back"

I headed back to town. In the meantime, I had asked Pastor Bolongwa to go downriver with the dugout and try to do something. I didn't know what, because the boat was so big and had no anchor, and no one else had one, either.

As I neared the service station, I saw my Portuguese friend. I stopped and told him my plight and asked again if there was any way we could fix his boat enough to go get ours.

He thought a minute and said, "Maybe, if you've got some cable."

I told him that I did indeed have some cable.

"Well, go get it and we'll try."

I got the cable, and we put it on his steering mechanism while he got his workmen to hook up the batteries. After nearly an hour of repair work, he said we were ready to go.

Just then, Pastor Bolongwa pulled up in the dugout to say that the workmen had finally succeeded in getting the boat to shore about six miles downstream. I heaved a sigh of relief, and off we went. The rescue was completed without incident, and we got back home about 7 P.M. with the boat.

Today I located a place to have the drive shaft replaced. If all goes well, it'll take only four days to get the new drive shaft installed.

Everything here is complicated. Sometimes life gets so ridiculous you just have to crack up and laugh to keep from crying. For example, in this city of 150,000 people there are no washers for sale to fix a leaky faucet! I ordered a 12-volt battery from Kinshasa six weeks ago and had it shipped by air. It took *one month* to get here by air (500 miles), and when it arrived it was busted all to pieces! I ordered 1,000 sacks of cement from Kinshasa over a month ago, and I learned today they haven't even been shipped yet! When we paid for the cement, we were told it would be put on the boat within two days. Now, our boat's broken down and I've got nothing for my crew of fourteen men to do. Can't make blocks—there's no cement. And can't haul sand—the boat's broken down.

I'm not crying on your shoulder. It's just that it's amazing how difficult it is to do anything here. And it's a tremendous, and I must say magnificent, challenge. Even if I sometimes get frustrated, I'm excited by all the problems and difficulties.

Your prayers are *needed*. Don't forget us—not even for one˙day!

P.S. My boat story does have a happy ending. On the way home late yesterday afternoon, under an incredible sky painted in blazing colors on the clouds by the setting sun, I asked my Portuguese friend what the charge was for getting the boat. I was really afraid to ask, because the whole trip had involved nearly four hours and lots of hard work.

In sharp contrast to the coldblooded greed I'd seen earlier in the day, he responded, "*Rien. Ce voyage est pour Dieu.*" (Nothing. This trip is for God.) And he wouldn't accept any pay for all his work and expense. A time like that makes all the frustrations worth while!

A few months later I had a totally different kind of day. It started, as usual, with my going to the Block and Sand Project for the morning worship service that begins our work. When I greeted Pastor Bolongwa, he responded with a downcast face.

"*J'ai les mauvaises nouvelles.* (I have bad news.)" He went on to tell me that the day before, the wife of one of his friends went out in a canoe with her son and they never returned home. Later in the afternoon, after a brief windstorm, the canoe, along with their clothes and papers, had washed ashore downstream. Everyone presumed them drowned, and at this very moment, he said, people were searching up and down the river for their bodies. Pastor Bolongwa's evident distress and his story touched my heart deeply. We had had so much death at that time. Mbomba, our newly engaged work foreman at the construction site, had lost a child just three weeks earlier, and the child of another workman had died the preceding week.

We had our usual song and prayer at the beginning of our work day, but when the prayer was finished, instead of giving my usual instructions for the day, I felt a strong urge to talk with the men about the fragility of life and about how a Christian should feel and think about death.

I began by referring to the missing woman and her son, and reminded the workmen that we never know when our lives will be snatched from us. Therefore, we should always live in a state of readiness for death. I went on to say that the death of loved ones always brings sadness, but beyond that sadness there should be real joy in knowing that Christ has brought us victory over death, and has assured us of a better home with God if we have loved Him and served Him with our lives here on earth. I said that all our fear of death should be swallowed up by a life of faith in God's promises for us. Death, I pointed out, is not the end, but is another beginning of life. I concluded my meditation by telling about my daughter Faith's singing "Happy Birthday" at Clarence Jordan's burial service.

I gave work instructions for the day, and left immediately on some errands in town. About two hours later, dark clouds came up which promised imminent rain. Since I was on the motorbike, I decided to try to beat the rain to the house. As I went along the river road, the wind started blowing with great force, causing the big trees that lined both sides of the road to sway dangerously. I was fearful that a great limb might come crashing down on me, but the drive went by without mishap and within a few minutes I was thankfully turning the corner into the long driveway leading to our house.

At that moment, two men ran up the driveway toward me, excitedly pointing toward the Block and Sand Project and yelling in Lingala. I slammed on the brakes and slid to a stop beside them.

"What is it?" I asked. "Talk to me in French. Speak in French!"

Finally they calmed down enough to exclaim, "*Un de vos travailleurs est décéde!* (One of your workers is dead!)"

"Who?" I yelled. But without waiting for an answer, I swung around and raced away.

I found all the men huddled around someone on the ground. They parted as I approached, and I saw one of the young workers, Mondonga, slumped on the earth. He was covered with blood, and there were two huge wounds in his head.

"What happened? What happened?"

Amid sobs, several of the men stammered that Mondonga had been outside the work shed, stacking blocks from the previous day, when without warning a big palm tree fell on top of him. They all thought he was dying.

Just at that moment, Linda rushed up in the car. Someone had gone for her just as I was coming in with the motorbike. We placed Mondonga gently in the car to take him to the hospital. As we did this, all of the men began wailing and crying as I had never seen grown men do before. It was a compassionate and unforgettable moment.

When we had Mondonga well situated in the hospital, I returned to the work site, where the men anxiously awaited news. In a quiet circle, I told them their friend was seriously injured, but I thought he would live. Pastor Bolongwa then prayed for him. He spoke of the fragility of life and referred to my meditation of that morning. My heart was very full, for I felt that I was a witness to, and a part of, something that was being orchestrated by God.

Afterwards, I went with some of the workmen to break the news to Mondonga's wife and to take her to the hospital. We learned then that he did not have a skull fracture, but that an arm and leg were broken, along with several ribs. Mondonga eventually recovered, after spending four months in the hospital and three more months at home. But he will walk with a limp for the rest of his life, for the leg that was smashed by the tree is now a few inches shorter than the other one.

(The other bad news of the day had a happier sequel. Two days later, after everyone had given them up for dead, the woman and son involved in the canoe accident were found safe and sound in a little village down the river. Somehow, they had made it to shore, and a family in mourning suddenly turned into one of great rejoicing.)

Another unexpected and dramatic episode concerning one of our workers began early one Saturday morning. As we were starting the worship period, our project mechanic walked up, disheveled and red-eyed from crying. He announced sadly that during the night his wife, seriously ill for several weeks, had died.

I dismissed the workers so they could go with him and prepare for the funeral. Other workers from the construction crew started making a coffin. I went to find a truck to take the body to the cemetery. When I drove up to the house, just before noon, there was a large crowd of people out front, dancing and beating drums. The men were covered with filth;

several of them were drunk. With our arrival (the construction project director and pastor were with me), the dancing stopped.

We gathered round and had Bible reading, some songs, and a prayer. I sensed there was unrest. After the service, one of our workers whispered to me that the family of the wife was angry at the husband because he had never paid for his wife. They were threatening to beat him. They also said they wouldn't allow the woman to be buried until he paid the bride price.

The situation began to heat up, as the men of the dead woman's family shouted louder and louder and finally hurled themselves at the mechanic. Our workers surrounded him—he was a very little man—trying to hold off his attackers. The poor mechanic didn't have any relatives in Mbandaka; his only family consisted of his friends at work.

The situation was worsening; I was afraid we were about to witness a killing. I shouted that I wanted to say something. Several of the people quieted down and gathered around me. I started talking about the International Year of Women that had just closed. (President Mobutu had put a lot of emphasis on this.) I said the purpose of this year dedicated to women was to elevate their status in the world. I pointed out that historically women had been considered inferior to men—objects useful only to bear children, cook meals, and plant gardens. They were like animals, to be bought and sold.

Then I reminded them that *all* black people in years past had been bought and sold. Slavery had been bad ... and it was stopped. People should never be treated as animals—all were created by God and are precious in His sight.

But even now, I said, you are still selling your women. That practice ought to be stopped. This dead woman, I said, is a human being. Was she paid for by her husband? I don't know. But you argue about whether she was paid for, and you propose to leave her out here to rot like a dead dog in the street. Is that any way to treat a human being? Let's bury her with dignity and deal with the other matters later.

I held my breath as the people looked at one another and began to talk among themselves. Then an older woman jumped forward and shouted that the woman must be buried. A few grumbled in the background, but the matter was ended. We quickly put her in the coffin, loaded it on the dump truck, and rolled off down the road to the cemetery. She was laid to rest without further incident, in a dignified and Christian manner.

I learned from Ikete, the project director, that the men were covered with filth from the toilet. This is a traditional custom to punish the husband and his friends for the death of the wife.

Our mechanic was a nominal Christian, but the family was not. This was the first funeral I had attended where the family was not Christian, and what a tremendous difference in the atmosphere and spirit. The Christians do not dirty themselves. They sing and dance, but it is not a dance of debauchery—it is a dancing of joy and celebration.

Some new problems began to arise at the Block and Sand Project which I unwittingly created. I had discovered that we could double our output of sand by installing floodlights on the shore and unloading at night. In this way, we could go out each morning, load up the barges with sand, unload at night, and go back the following day for more. The former practice had been to go out for sand one day and unload the next, returning for more sand the third day. But I didn't anticipate the reactions this method would produce.

First of all, fishermen on the river (who do most of their fishing at night) would come by in their dugouts and yell at our workers, asking why they weren't home in bed.

"Daytime is the time for working. Nighttime is for sleeping. Go home! Go to bed!" they yelled. (Apparently the fact that they also worked at night never occurred to them.)

Our workers would yell back at them to shut up and mind their own business. "We're making our living. Leave us alone."

But the fishermen kept yelling, and there were several near fights. Finally I told our workmen to ignore the taunts and to make absolutely no reply. Over a period of time, this problem subsided.

Then one night the military arrived.

"All of you are under arrest!" the soldier announced.

"Why?"

"For working at night."

I was asleep when one of the workmen banged on our roof with a long stick, shouting "*Patron. Patron!* Come quickly!"

"What's broken now?" I wondered, as I slipped on my pants.

When I opened the door, all the workmen were standing solemn-faced on the porch. A soldier looked sternly at them and then at me.

"What is it?" I asked.

"I've arrested these men for working at night," he replied.

"You've done *what?*"

"I've arrested these men for working at night. That's against the law."

"Against what law?"

"Against the law of the Government."

"Working at night is not against the law," I assured him.

I didn't know that for a fact, but I felt fairly certain there was no such law, and that if I spoke firmly enough he might believe me. I thought that he was acting on his own. He had never seen anyone working at night, so he assumed it was against the law. Besides, if he precipitated a problem, he might think he would get a bribe.

"Look, friend," I said. "These men are working at night because I told them to. I am responsible. If someone has broken the law, it is not these men. They are just following my instructions. Now, they've got work to do. We are working for the betterment of your community and your country. Everything we are doing is to help the people. We plan to get the Block and Sand Project in good running condition and then we will start building houses for families that need them. You know what a problem housing is in Mbandaka, don't you?"

"Yes, it is a big problem."

"And that is not the only problem," I continued. "There are many other problems. To solve them, it is necessary to work a lot. More people ought to be working at night. When one has big problems, it is necessary to work overtime to solve them. Men, go back down there and unload the rest of that sand. I will take care of this matter with the soldier myself."

With a casual wave of my hand, I sent the men back to work, and continued my monologue with the soldier without allowing him time to countermand my instructions. In actual fact, he didn't even try. We stood on the porch for another twenty minutes or so, becoming better buddies all the time. Finally we were laughing together. I put my arm around his shoulders and we walked up the road a way. Then we shook hands. He left; the men went on working; I went back to sleep.

That was not the end of our problems from working at night, however. A week later, another soldier came and "rearrested" the men. We went through the same routine all over again, and finally he also left.. But then men began to be arrested on the way home after work. They would be stopped and questioned about why they were out on the roads so late at night. For this problem, we had certificates of service made up and signed by a church authority stating that the man was an employee of the Block and Sand Project and that his work was unloading sand at night. These certificates helped, but did not entirely correct the situation.

Finally one night some soldiers arrested a man (not one of our workers) and beat him to death. This caused such an uproar in town that the government authorities strictly forbade the soldiers to harass people with arrests on their way home from work.

Only once in three years did we have to pay a fine (and that time one of our drivers had clearly violated the law), but we wasted untold hours and energy walking up and down the road with soldiers and sitting in military offices "arranging" violations. And we never paid a bribe, even though one was requested on several occasions.

In spite of the many unexpected delays and frustrations, we managed to make steady progress. By the end of 1973 we had repaired the boat and the conveyor belt. We were regularly hauling sand to make blocks and to supply customers. We had made minor repairs on the block-making machine, and it was turning out more and more blocks every week. We had made another five hundred planks for these blocks, to replace the ones eaten by termites. The old truck had received new tires and some much-needed repairs, and the major repair work on the sand barges was under way. In addition, we were making enough money to pay the workers regularly with some left over as profit!

We were now ready to turn our attention toward the beginning of our long-awaited housing venture.

6
Bokotola

WE sat in a plush, air-conditioned government office. Across the desk from us an imposing official wearing an immaculate black Zaire suit, a colorful scarf knotted about his neck, studied our request. We watched him hopefully, trying to analyze his expression as he read the Memorandum. Both sides of his broad, shiny-black face were laced with big, protruding scars, carefully carved many years earlier to identify him as a member of his particular tribe.

Now, high in his country's administration and with an office in the capital building of Equator Region in the city of Mbandaka, he had the authority to grant or to deny us a parcel of land for a housing project to be sponsored and built by the Church of Christ in Zaire. (In Zaire fifty-three Protestant bodies, called "communities," are united under the name of *Eglise du Christ au Zaire* [Church of Christ in Zaire].) My companions were Pastor Elonda, president of the Church Synod for Equator Region, and Ikete, Projects Director of the Disciples Community.

I had arrived in Mbandaka with my wife Linda and our four children on July 3, 1973. For two months I had labored steadily to put the church-operated Block and Sand Project—the only enterprise manufacturing cement building blocks in this teeming city of 150,000—into good working condition.

Now I had felt satisfied enough about the condition of the Project to propose to church leaders that we attempt a housing program. They were immediately enthusiastic, and had asked me to prepare a Memorandum for the government authorities asking for land and for assistance in laying out streets.

A week later we, with our Memorandum, were admitted into the office of the Regional Commissioner.

MEMORANDUM TO: Citoyen* Ngoma Ntoto Mbwangi
                Commissaire Régional de l'Equateur
DATE: September 24, 1973
SUBJECT: 1) Block and Sand Project of the Church of Christ at Mbandaka
         2) Proposed Project to build 100 houses.
         3) Request for plot of land for the aforesaid 100 houses, and assistance in laying out streets, installing drainage systems, etc.

*In Zaire, by governmental decree, everyone is addressed by the French word for "citizen."

In 1966 my wife and I made an extensive tour of five African countries to visit church projects and missionary enterprises. We spent two weeks in Zaire (then Congo), and in that short time were deeply impressed with your beautiful country and your warm and friendly people. The visit to your country, including a stay in Mbandaka, was the highlight of our voyage. We were impressed too, by the potential here, for truly God has blessed you with a land rich in natural resources. It remains now to develop these resources for the betterment of all the people.

We were pleased to see that the church in your Region was becoming involved in that process. This is proper, for the church is devoted to bringing "Good News" to people about the good life God has planned in the far reaches of eternity and also about the good life God desires for His people here and now. Jesus said, "I came that they might have life, and that they might have it more abundantly."

We were specifically interested in the *Project du Briques et Sable* (Block and Sand Project) which the church was just beginning to operate. In fact, when I returned to the United States I raised funds to purchase a dump truck for the project.

In my country I have been a businessman and a lawyer, but recently I have devoted my time to development work in poverty areas. In 1967 I launched a fund-raising program for a struggling college for black Americans in a Southern state. In 1968 I helped launch, and then became director of, a program in the state of Georgia called Koinonia Partners. This Christian organization is largely devoted to development work as an imperative of the Christian faith—establishing rural industries to give employment to poor people, operating extensive farming programs, and building houses for low-income families.

During the time I was director of this program, we built more than thirty houses. The building is continuing at the present time, with new houses being finished at the rate of one or two a month. Approximately forty houses have now been completed in two locations.

Late last year, my wife and I decided to return to your country to assist the church in Equator Region with its development program. We contacted the Disciples of Christ in the United States and they agreed to sponsor us here for a two- or three-year period.

We arrived in Mbandaka on July 3, 1973, and I immediately began a study of the various projects of the church. The conclusion of this study was that the one with the greatest potential was the Block and Sand Project. Accordingly, I requested permission to be the director of this project for an interim period for the purpose of establishing it as a viable enterprise.

In this connection, I immediately began to seek funds from sources in the United States in order to replace the project's worn-out equipment. I have already received a firm commitment from the United Church Board for World Ministries in the United States for a gift of $5,000 to be used in buying new equipment and making repairs. I expect to receive additional grants to the amount of approximately $10,000 to $20,000. With this money we will purchase badly needed items, make repairs on the dump truck, barges, crane, and other equipment, and put the project in good operating condition.

Even now, with the old equipment and with many problems, the project is beginning to function much better. During my first month as director (August 16 to September 15) we produced 7,578 cement blocks and hauled 62 truckloads of sand. With better facilities this production can be at least tripled. With the Block and Sand Project in good operating condition, we will be ready to launch the second significant development project—the building of houses.

I don't think I need to elaborate on the need for housing in Mbandaka. It is evident to even a casual observer that literally thousands of people live in inadequate homes. The project herein proposed, even though large in scope, will fill but a fraction of the total need. But it is a beginning, and I believe it will inspire others to do likewise both here and in other cities. The project will be highly visible and will attract visitors from near and far. Some of them will doubtless be provoked into action of a similar nature elsewhere.

The funding agency for the houses we built in Georgia is called "The Fund for Humanity." This Fund received its money from churches and individuals who wanted to share with people less fortunate than themselves. I have proposed such a Fund here, and the leadership of the church has wholeheartedly endorsed the idea. The Fund will be administered by the church, under the direction of a committee of managers numbering three to five persons. I will initially be the director of the Fund, but upon my departure another person within the church will assume this responsibility. Koinonia Partners, Inc., the aforementioned organization in Georgia, has already promised a grant of $3,000 to establish this Fund. Other individuals and organizations will be making grants within the near future. By January I expect to have $15,000 to $40,000 with which to begin the project.

The leadership of the church proposes that we plan for the construction of 100 houses in one central location in the city. These houses would be built of concrete blocks with a concrete floor, tin roof, and outdoor kitchen and toilet. We expect the cost of each house to be in the range of Z1,000 to Z3,000.*

Each family would be expected to make a down payment of Z100, and each month thereafter they would pay approximately Z4 to Z12 back into the Fund for Humanity for a period of twenty years, *without interest*, until the house was completely paid for. But each family would also be encouraged to donate to the Fund for Humanity each month to the extent of their ability in order to help others get a better house as they have been helped. This feature of the plan encourages sharing and concern for others which is at the core of the Christian faith, and it also builds up the country by getting people interested in helping their fellow men. The people of the church in Equator Region will also be encouraged to share in the cost of this project.

The committee of managers for the Fund for Humanity will interview and select the families to occupy the houses and will establish the monthly payments. This committee will also designate the person to receive the payments and deposit them into the Fund for Humanity account.

*When we first arrived in Zaire the official exchange rate was 1 Zaire = 2 dollars. Later the exchange rate was allowed to float, and it averaged about 1 Zaire = $1.10. So for simplicity, throughout this book I have assumed the ratio 1 Zaire = 1 dollar.

Finally, let me point out that the housing program will provide a steady source of business to the Block and Sand Project, helping to ensure its continuity. As you know, this project is the only one of its kind in the area and is vitally needed for the continuing development of the city and Equator Region.

Therefore, on behalf of the leadership of the church, I would like to request: 1) a plot of land suitable for the erection of 100 houses, and 2) assistance from the appropriate governmental agency to cut streets, install drainage systems, and so on. All of this work need not be done at the beginning, but can be continued as the construction of the houses progresses.

In conclusion, let me remind you that God has expressed His love for us clearly in the person of Jesus Christ, and we are commanded to show our love for each other in a similar way. I know that you have a love and concern for your people, and together we can give expression to this.

> (*Signed*) Millard Fuller
> For the Church of Christ of Zaire—Mbandaka

The Commissioner read silently for several long minutes. He looked up and seemed to be staring past us. He gazed out the window. Then he read some more. Finally, he spoke. "I see here that you expect to get certain funds for this project, but how much money do you have *now*, with which to begin and continue the work?"

All of us squirmed. This was the question we had feared. We didn't have any money. Would the Government grant land with such a nebulous possibility of funds, no assured money, and nothing in hand?

Pastor Elonda spoke first. "Mr. Fuller has experience in developing such projects. He started such a venture in the United States, as explained in the Memorandum, which was built from the beginning on donated funds. The money came in as the building progressed. He believes that if we can secure land here and get started, the needed funds will come."

The Commissioner gazed out the window again for a long minute. Then he fixed me with an expressionless stare. He waited for me to speak.

My beginner's French was about to get its acid test. I searched for just the right words to give him the convincing answer necessary. "*Oui, c'est vrai* (Yes, it is true). We don't have any money. But we have faith that God will provide it."

I went on to explain that I knew numerous people of faith and compassion in the United States and elsewhere who would want to help us if we got something started, and that I firmly believed that God, through them and others, would provide the funds. I also told him I thought we could generate profits from the Block and Sand Project, and that all of this money could be put into the Fund for Humanity for building houses.

He listened intently, and asked a few more questions of Pastor Elonda and Ikete. Then he addressed us.

"We all know what a tremendous problem we have here in Mbandaka with inadequate housing. We want to encourage anyone who can help solve it. That's why I am sympathetic toward your desire to develop a housing center. The only question is the uncertainty of your funding. In spite of that, I am inclined to think that your request will be granted. We will give you our answer within a few days. In the meantime, I am going to call the Survey Office and arrange for you to go over there and decide with them what land is available and suitable for your proposed project."

He picked up the phone and called the Survey Office of the city of Mbandaka. In a few concise sentences he explained to the director that we were in his office talking about a housing project, that he was inclined to grant our request for land for one hundred houses, and that he was sending us to the Survey Office for help in locating a desirable building site.

He stood up as he replaced the telephone. Smiling broadly, he extended his hand to each of us. We were dismissed.

As we clattered down the stairs and out of the building, I asked, "Well, what do you think?" Pastor Elonda didn't hesitate even a second. "We've got the land! Let's go choose the site."

I had already decided on the site that I hoped was available. It was in almost the geographic center of the city—a large open tract covered with scrub bushes, palm trees ... and twenty-foot-high anthills! It was bordered on one side by the grounds of the General Hospital of Mbandaka and on another by the *Avenue de la Révolution;* across the avenue stood the largest and most beautiful Protestant church in the city. And it was close enough to the block-making plant to make hauling supplies convenient. There were only two questions in my mind about this land. First, it seemed low, and I feared we might have problems with drainage. And second, I wondered why such a large section of land remained undeveloped right in the heart of the city.

When we arrived at the Survey Office, we were met by Director Bakabubu, a little round-faced man who was most anxious to be helpful. I described the tract of land we preferred and he sent an assistant scurrying to the dusty stack of maps to find one for that area of the city. Within a couple of minutes the assistant returned. The director studied the map for a minute and then announced with a smile, "Yes, that area belongs to the State and has not been reserved for anything. It is available so far as we are concerned."

"Excellent," I said. "Let's go look it over."

We quickly piled into our car and drove the short distance to the site. After wading through weeds and grass higher than our heads, maneuvering around huge anthills, and jumping over ditches and water puddles for the next half hour, I was ready to say that we definitely wanted that land. It was unquestionably low-lying land, but I felt we could solve that problem.

"We would like to request this site," I said to Director Bakabubu.

"Okay," he replied. "But before you make your final decision, let's look at some more land that is available."

For the next couple of hours we drove through the city looking at other sites, but I never wavered from my belief that the first place was the right one.

In a few days the appropriate letters of request were written, and before the end of the month we received assurance that the land would be given to us *without cost*. The official letter granting the property to the church was not prepared until January, but with this verbal guarantee we were ready to go to work.

My friend Don Mosley, director of Koinonia Partners and a capable surveyor-engineer-builder, had been in close contact with me since our arrival in Zaire, and had expressed lively interest in what we were dreaming about. So, on October 1, 1973, I wrote him as follows:

Here is the plan for the housing development. We're getting all the property within the dark blue lines. As it is presently plotted, there are enough lots for ninety houses. But we've gotten permission from the government to change the plan as we see fit. The land is almost totally flat and unfortunately low, but a system of small drainage ditches seems to be keeping the lots dry. A big drainage ditch runs along the right side.

I would like your ideas on rearranging this plot. How would you like to come out here in January or February to help me lay this thing off on the ground and get it started?

On October 25, Don replied enthusiastically:

Get a room ready for me, partner—because I'm on my way! I can leave right after Christmas, and will probably arrive about the first of January. Four weeks should be enough time—if you have surveying equipment—for us to work out the details of the subdivision, get at least its principal points staked out accurately, and maybe draw up some house plans (with a chance for me to get an idea at first hand of climatic conditions, prevailing family patterns, use of space, ideas about privacy, etc.).

If you know of anyone who would be likely to help with ticket money, send me their names. I'm assuming if I raise enough cash to get to Mbandaka and back, you'll have a place lined up for me to stay and eat while I'm there. That fair enough?

Fair enough, indeed! Within a few weeks Don and I together had secured the fare from a most ecumenical group—a Methodist church in Coral Gables, Florida, a Southern Baptist church in Tampa, and a Hutterite Community in North Dakota. Don's father, in Waco, Texas, who was getting more and more interested in the project, put in the last couple of hundred dollars. Don would land in Kinshasa on December 31, and come up to Mbandaka by river boat a few days later.

In the meantime I was looking for a builder—and for building money. In late September, I had visited Vern Preheim, Zaire director of the Mennonite Central Committee. I had explained the proposed project and requested MCC to send us some builders. Vern was supportive and encouraging from the start, and he began immediately to search for help for us.

In December, Vern wrote:

Dan Froese, who has been at Kikwit for twenty months, would like very much to come and help you. He speaks very good Kituba, and Rev. Elonda thinks he would pick up Lingala very fast, as they are quite similar. Dan is a farm lad from Saskatchewan, Canada, and thus has a good general background in both mechanics and construction. ... If you are willing to accept him for three months minimum and possibly longer, send me a radio message. He is in Kinshasa and could come right away.

Dan arrived on December 21; and the same day he fixed a pesky oil leak in our block-making machine. The following week he started making doors and windows for the first house in the project, although we were far from ready even to lay the first foundation. And when Don Mosley arrived two weeks later, Dan plunged in with him to survey the land.

When Don first arrived in Mbandaka I took him to the Survey Office and introduced him to Citizen Bakabubu, the director, in hopes we could borrow some surveying equipment. The church had an old surveying instrument, but Don doubted its accuracy.

Director Bakabubu did not hesitate a minute.

"Yes, we have surveying equipment. I'll have someone fetch it. You may choose what you want to work with."

An assistant returned shortly thereafter with three brand-new Swiss-made theodolites that had never been out of their cases. There were also new tripods and surveying rods—the very best of everything we needed. Don was amazed, the more so as he examined the tools and realized how sophisti-

cated they were. He had expected to come to the middle of
Africa and work with ancient equipment—or perhaps with
nothing. He had already thought of ways to improvise. Instead, he had been provided with the most modern surveying
gear he had ever seen.

Don Mosley and Dan Froese made a great surveying team.
Don operated the theodolite while Dan crashed through the
bushes, going forward, backward, right and left, placing the
surveying rods as Don indicated with wide sweeping motions
of his hands. The job was a big one. We knew Don would have
to work fast to finish it during his brief three weeks' stay. We
began having an early breakfast each morning so that he and
Dan could get started shortly after daylight. Often they
worked until it was too dark to see anything through the surveying instrument. Then they would drag themselves home,
to start again the following morning.

Our biggest problem in the surveying was clearing "lines of
sight." Weeds, bushes, a scattering of palm trees, and scores
of giant anthills blanketed the property. It was impossible to
sight from one point to another with the theodolite.

I went to see the Mayor of Mbandaka and explained the
situation, asking that the city furnish us some men. The mayor
already knew about the project and was willing to help. So, for
the next couple of weeks we had thirty to fifty men at our
disposal armed with machetes, *coup-coups** and shovels to cut
down trees and greenery blocking our lines of sight, and to dig
through the huge anthills. The work moved ahead rapidly with
their aid.

In the meantime, I continued the search for money.
Koinonia Partners had established the Mbandaka Fund for
Humanity in October with a $3,000 gift. Later in the same
month Margaret Gage, a friend in California, added $1,000.

In September, I received a letter from P. V. George, pastor
of the Plymouth Congregational Church, Plymouth, New
Hampshire: "How much money would it take to build a house
in the project? ... We find the Spirit leading us in this direction
and we shall move as soon as we hear from you ... "

They heard from me immediately—I always answer such
letters promptly! And they moved. In January we received
their first check, and in March I was able to write, "Last week
we dug the foundation for *your* house. We've got our blocks
and doors already made. So we're on the way—and you are a
large part of making all this possible. It sure is exciting, and I
hope all of you share in this joy and exhilaration."

During these early months of the project we received several other welcome gifts from individuals and churches. One of
these gifts came from Sam Emerick, director of the

*Knives with long, thin, slightly curved blades used to cut grass.

Yokefellow Institute in Richmond, Indiana. I had come to know Sam a few years earlier when he had participated in a thinking and planning session at Koinonia with Clarence Jordan, about a dozen other men, and myself, that launched the ministry of Koinonia Partners and established the Fund for Humanity. The following year I was with Sam again when Clarence Jordan and I conducted a Discipleship School at the Institute. I now sent a letter of thanks to him for his generous personal gift.

Later, his response just about floored me when I opened it. "You didn't know it, Millard, but I've been working for the Lilly Endowment here in Indianapolis since November, in the Religion Division. I've been excited about what you are doing, and I have explored ways to help. The Endowment has approved $25,000 for your project."

This was exactly the boost we needed. Don Mosley, working with Dan Froese, had completed the survey work in January and had put in permanent concrete boundary markers for the outside limits of the building site. A total of 114 lots were platted for the project. Dan had worked during the month of February preparing our main access road and clearing the first ten building lots with a bulldozer the Government had put at our disposal. Boundary markers were then put in for these first ten lots. We had received the official letter from the Government in January granting the property to the church. And we had started building the first two houses.

People in the area had told me the name of our property was *"Bokotola,"* which meant "man who does not care for others." I wondered why it had been given this name, and why the site had never been developed. All the land around it was covered with houses, a hospital, markets, schools, and other buildings. At first I had thought it was because our section was low and swampy. But then I realized that all the surrounding land was equally low, and that it was easily drainable. I kept wondering about this for several months.

When the church in Equator Region had its General Assembly meeting in July, Dr. Bokeleale, the national president of the Church of Christ of Zaire, was invited to speak. I knew he was a native of Mbandaka, so one evening when he visited our home for dinner I asked him if he knew the history of Bokotola and why it was never developed.

"Ye-e-esss," he intoned, leaning far back in his chair and stretching his arms up over his head, "that strip of land was the dividing section between the Africans and the whites in colonial days."

He went on to tell us how the Africans were restricted to one side, while the Belgians and other whites lived on the other side. It was absolutely illegal for an African to live on the Belgians' side. As he spoke, this whole thing suddenly exploded in my mind and in Dr. Bokeleale's too, as it dawned on us just what a highly significant and symbolic act the church had undertaken. In the name of Christ, the one who cares the most for others, we were covering Bokotola with houses for people in need. In the name of Christ, the one who came to break down walls of separation between man and man, and man and God, we were going to eliminate forever this old segregation barrier by covering it with a sparkling Christian community.

7

A Growing Community

"TWENTY-FIVE thousand Zaires!" I couldn't believe what I'd just read. "You want 25,000 Zaires for a building permit? You want 25,000 Zaires to give us permission to build those houses? That's 50,000 dollars!* You must be kidding!"

Just a few minutes before, I had walked out the front door of the church administrative building on this clear morning in early February of 1974. I was feeling good. Things were beginning to fall into place with the housing project. Don Mosley had completed the survey in January and had returned to Koinonia. A few days later, we had finally received the official letter granting us the tract of thirty-five acres for the houses. The Government had given us the use of a bulldozer, and Dan Froese was out at the site at this very moment, opening our main access road and leveling some of the 20-foot-high anthills. Within a few days we'd be ready to start the first house.

As I had left the building, Pastor Boyaka had called to me from under a nearby tree. "Come over here, please." He was standing beside a well-dressed young man who was holding an official-looking piece of paper. "Mr. Fuller, this man has a bill for you."

The paper was shoved into my hand. At a glance I saw it was a bill from the city government office responsible for issuing building permits. We had applied for an *autorisation de bâtir* (authorization to build) soon after receiving verbal assurances that we would be granted the land for the housing project. We had expected this permit to be either free of charge or certainly no more than a few Zaires. But as my eyes focused on the figures on the paper I suddenly felt sick. There it was, and unmistakably clear:

"Building Permit . . . . Z25,000"

"Twenty-five thousand Zaires! are they kidding?" I looked at Pastor Boyaka and his companion.

"No," Pastor Boyaka replied. "He says that is the fee for the permits on the 114 houses we intend to build."

"Well, Pastor," I replied, "we need to make arrangements for my airplane ticket home. This kills the project. We can't pay that amount of money for a building permit. That's ridiculous. We're having a hard time just finding enough money to build the houses. We certainly couldn't dig up an

*At the official exchange rate in 1974.

additional 25,000 Zaires to throw away on a building permit!"
The young man looked quite concerned. "You mean you are going to abandon the project and return to America?"
"That's right, friend. I came out here to work with development. I wanted to build some houses to alleviate the tremendous problem you have with inadequate housing. But if you are going to slap us with ridiculous fees like this, there is no way we can continue. We'll just quit. That's all we can do. You have killed the project."

Pastor Boyaka chimed in, "That's right, Citoyen, we can't pay a fee like that. Why can't you bill us one house at a time as we start them?"

"Okay," the young man responded quickly. "We can do that."

"No, it's not okay," I rejoined. "That's still too much. We are building 114 houses and you want a total of 25,000 Zaires. That's over 200 Zaires a house. We can't accept that."

Without hesitation he asked, "Would you be willing to pay 10 Zaires a house for a building permit?"

Again I couldn't believe my ears. Here he was going from 25,000 Zaires to 200 to 10 within a matter of minutes. I decided to go for nothing.

"That's still too much," I said. "I don't understand why you should charge anything. This is a nonprofit project of the church, designed to help people who don't have adequate lodging. You should be giving *us* money instead of asking for it. We don't feel that we should pay anything for the building permit."

The young man lowered his head and shuffled his feet in the dust. "I don't know about that," he said. "You should pay something for a building permit for those houses."

"Look," I said, "if it is necessary to pay a small fee, we won't object. Go back to your office and work something out. Then bill us as we start the houses. We'll pay. But please do issue the papers to enable us to begin construction. Our entrance road will be finished within a few days, and we want to get the first house under way."

"Agreed," he responded. "I'll get something worked out and have your building permit issued within a few days."

He walked away. Pastor Boyaka and I looked at each other and sighed with relief.

"That man scared the daylights out of me," I groaned. "I sure thought he had killed Bokotola!"

A few days later I saw Pastor Boyaka and asked if he had heard any more from the building permit man. When he replied that he hadn't, I decided we should get in touch with the man, because we were almost ready to start construction.

The contacts started. Over the next three weeks we must have gone to that office at least fifteen times. Always the response was the same: "Come back later; we still haven't had time to prepare the papers."

My patience wore thin. I told Pastor Boyaka I wanted to start building.

"No," he replied, "it would be too risky without the written permit in our hands. Wait a few more days."

So I waited, and waited. Then it was nearly March. We were ready to pour the first foundation; still there was no building permit.

"Dan," I said, "we're going to start—building permit or not. Start digging the foundation."

Within a few days we had the first foundation dug. Then we started pouring cement.

On the second day, a man drove up in the church car. The driver announced in a loud voice, "Monsieur Fuller, Pastor Boyaka would like to see you immediately at his house. Do you want to go back with me?"

"No, I'll be there in just a minute on my motorbike."

When I rolled up in front of the pastor's house, he was standing in the front yard with Pastor Mpombo, the auxiliary bishop of the Disciples Church in Equator Region. Pastor Boyaka looked concerned. "I hear you've started building."

"That's right. We're pouring the foundation for the first house."

"But we don't have a building permit. You are moving too fast."

"Yes, Monsieur Fuller," chimed in Pastor Mpombo, "you must remember that you are in Zaire. We move slowly here."

I was hot and tired from working in the blazing sun. I had become more and more frustrated with the slow progress we were making—and now I was being criticized for going too fast! Anger welled up within me.

"Too fast!" I yelled. "I think we're going too slow. I didn't come to Zaire to fritter away my time. I thought you wanted help with development. I intend to get something accomplished during my brief stay here. If that's not possible, I'll go home. You can look for someone else who will be content to diddle away his time. Either you are going to let me move ahead with my work or I'll call it quits. The Government gave us that land explicitly for building houses—now they won't let us do it. That's totally illogical!"

A long discussion followed—during which time I cooled down—and we arrived at a decision. We would pour foundations, but would not start putting up walls until we got the building permit. In that way, nothing would be visible. In the meantime, Pastor Boyaka would make a dedicated effort to secure the building permit as quickly as possible. I returned to the site and work continued.

Several days went by. We had two foundations finished and were starting on the third. I wanted to start the walls. I went to see Pastor Boyaka. No, he hadn't yet gotten the permit. Yes, you can start the walls, but build them only to a height of five or six blocks.

In the weeks that followed, we dug and poured more foundations and put the walls up, little by little, higher and higher. Finally the first house was roofed and completely finished. Then the second ... and the third.

Months went by ... a year ... two years. Eventually all 114 foundations were poured; hundreds of people moved in; but no building permit was ever issued. And we never paid a cent for the privilege of building.

Unofficially, the first house was for Lokesa, our *cuisinier*. In Zaire, all domestic workers are men, and whatever their responsibilities, their title is "cook." Lokesa had been working for another missionary family, which was leaving; so we hired him to help Linda prepare the noon meals and do the weekly wash.

The very first day Lokesa worked for us, he gave me 60 Zaires to keep for him. He told me he had been saving that money for several years (adding a little to it whenever he could) to build a house. He knew nothing of our hopes for a housing project.

A few days later, Linda and I visited him at his home, a classic scene of Zaire poverty. The house was made of mud, with a palm-leaf roof that was caving in. There were just two tiny rooms for Lokesa, his wife, and their four children. The house was so small they could only sleep in it; at other times they had to stay outside.

I then told Lokesa of the possibility of building up the Block and Sand Project and launching a housing program. I promised him that if we were able to realize that dream, I would arrange for him to get the very first house. He was ecstatic with joy. "Heee-heee-heeee!" He laughed on and on. Lokesa had a weird, wailing laugh that was undoubtedly the one of its kind in the world. "*Patron*, if you start building houses, you'll have so many customers you won't know what to do. *Everybody* wants a house!"

Lokesa's words proved prophetic. Within a few months after launching Bokotola, we had received over 3,000 written requests for houses, and hundreds of people were streaming to our door to tell us about their pressing need for a house!

But we had to begin gradually. As funds were donated to the Mbandaka Fund for Humanity, I would first buy cement. Some of this cement would be used for foundations and floors, but over 90 per cent of it would go into concrete blocks. Then we would sell about half of the blocks to the public at a profit, using the remaining half in the construction work at Bokotola. In this way, I could significantly multiply each gift before using it at the construction site. During the first 28 months we were building at Bokotola (March 1974 to July 1976), we purchased over a thousand tons of cement and manufactured nearly half a million concrete blocks. We also sold about half of the sand we took from the river bottom. All these profits went directly into the Fund for Humanity in order to build more houses.

In mid-1974 our block-and-sand business received three big boosts. First, an English construction company came to town to rebuild the runway and erect several buildings at the Mbandaka airport. We made a deal with them to furnish most of their sand and all of their blocks. This gave us a significant source of income for over a year. Second, construction began on a new hotel in Mbandaka and we were able to provide a lot of the materials. Third was the building of a new radio station shortly thereafter, and again we furnished the blocks. All of these projects, in addition to our regular stream of customers, provided thousands of dollars for Bokotola. To keep up with the demand, we doubled our work force at the Block and Sand Project to a total of twenty-eight men and added to the night crew for unloading the sand.

Unfortunately our work force was not always occupied. The Zairois have an incredible number of holidays, the origins of which were frequently puzzling. Generally they seemed to fall into four categories:

1. *Official national holidays.* These included nine days a year celebrating some event in the political life of the country (religious holidays had been abandoned). For example, May 20 was the anniversary of the *Mouvement Populaire de la Révolution* (the political party of Zaire); October 27 marked the day on which the name of the country had been changed to Zaire, and November 24 marked the coming to power of President Mobutu.

2. *Presidential visits.* These dates were uncertain, but each year we could count on a few. The pattern was always the same. An announcement would be made that the President would arrive in town on a certain day. "*Salongo* (public work day)" would be ordered. Offices, businesses, stores—every-

thing would be ordered to close. Everybody must go out on the streets and roads and clean up, cut weeds, fill in potholes, clear away trash, in order to make the city beautiful for the President. Excitement would fill the air as the day arrived for his visit, and again everything would close down. Everybody would be ordered to go to the airport or to the river port, depending on how he was supposed to arrive, to greet him ... and then he wouldn't come.

Soon word would circulate that he would come two days later. Stores would reopen and work would continue for the following two days; then, once again, everything must close down and everybody must go to greet the President. Perhaps he would come. Perhaps not. If not, another date would be set and the procedure of closing down and walking to the port to greet him would be repeated.

If the President's stay in town was short, everything would remain closed until he left. If the visit was for several days, work would recommence and stores would open until word came that he would leave on a certain day. Then all work would stop again and everyone would be ordered to go to the appropriate port to wave good-bye to him ... and then he wouldn't leave.

Another date would be set for his departure. Again everything must close down and everyone must walk to the port once more. The airport was at least five miles from the center of town. For people who lived on the other side of the city, the walk could be ten miles or more each way. Only a tiny fraction of the population had any means of transportation other than their feet, and after three or four forced walks of ten to twenty miles each, there was universal fatigue, and work suffered for several days afterwards.

To the Western mind all this rigamarole seems utterly ridiculous, but the Zairois, for the most part, didn't seem to mind it. I asked a group of men one day about this. They replied that in their culture total respect is given to the chief. It would be considered grossly impolite for any "chief" to visit and not be properly greeted by absolutely everyone when he arrived. The same is true when he departs. The men compared the situation to the arrival of the grandfather of a family. When someone's father arrives from his village, it is expected that the family's activities will cease and that they will all visit with him, sharing the news and mininstering completely to him, until he is settled and comfortable. Only then can household activities return to normal. For a wife or a child to continue working or playing when granddad arrives or when he departs would be considered a crowning insult.

On one visit to Mbandaka in 1975, President Mobutu felt

that he did not receive a suitable welcome, so he left and came back again a few days later to be properly received. Feverish activity went on all over town in the meantime. School classes were dismissed and the students were obliged to dance and sing praises to the President for one whole day. The following day, all government workers were made to sing and dance for the chief. When he came the second time the crowd was enormous, and the President was satisfied.

On one occasion we got word that the President would visit Bokotola. Through Dr. Bokeleale, the national president of the Church of Christ in Zaire, he had given three thousand Zaires' to the project and had spoken favorably of it in a nationwide radio broadcast. Now he was coming to town, and a visit to the project was on his itinerary. So we got busy. A big welcoming sign swung over the main entrance street. Hundreds of palm branches were cut and staked along both sides of the street leading into the community. A large display of all the house designs and a map of the housing area were prepared. Then the day before the scheduled visit to Mbandaka, the President of Chad was killed. This delayed the trip for a week. All the palm branches withered; we cut more and replaced them. A week later, President Mobutu arrived in the city, and we got a new itinerary giving the date of his visit to Bokotola.

Finally the big day arrived. Thousands of people poured into Bokotola to greet the President. Groups of colorful dancers rolled in on army trucks and started singing and dancing. More truckloads of armed soldiers arrived. Regional officials and church leaders came. The stage was set to receive the President.

He didn't come. Just before noon, a big black car rolled in and an important-looking man stepped out and talked to one of the local officials already there; then he got back in the car and roared away. He had brought the message that the President would visit the project two days later. Word spread quickly, and the crowd melted away into the surrounding neighborhoods.

The following day we tried to carry on normal work, but that was practically impossible. Everyone thought only of the forthcoming presidential visit. The next morning people again poured in by the thousands. The dancers came, and the soldiers, and the important-looking officials, and the church leaders. Pastor Boyaka had his speech for the President all prepared for delivery as he stepped from his limousine. He would be there at 9 A.M.

He didn't come. A message was sent: he will arrive at ten-thirty. He didn't show up. Another big black car appeared— now it was definite. He would be there at noon. Everybody got into place; the dancers lined up in perfect order along with the soldiers.

Finally the moment arrived. In just a minute or two he would make his entrance. People craned their necks; they could hear a vehicle approaching. He's coming! But it wasn't his vehicle.

Twelve-thirty came. One o'clock. One-thirty. A few people started leaving. Then more. Some of the officials left. I left. The mass exodus was under way again. Bokotola returned to normal, minus a presidential visit.

The next day we learned that he had secretly left town at midmorning of the previous day. People said he had visited Bokotola at midnight of the night before; however, no one knew for sure. What I did know was that we had lost over a thousand man-hours of work—but in Zaire one is not supposed to think about things like that!

3. *Salongo.* This is a Lingala word which means "father of the hoe." Under Mobutu, *Salongo* has come to mean any clean-up work imposed by the Government. In addition to *salongo* prior to an announced presidential visit, other days were so designated from time to time, frequently without warning. During one period of several weeks, *salongo* was held every Saturday. At another time it was every Wednesday. Sometimes we would arrive at work and receive the message that the day had just been declared "Salongo Day." Everyone was to return home and prepare to clean up a certain area of the community. Soon hundreds of people could be seen swinging machetes, *coup-coups*, hoes and shovels, up and down the streets.

One Saturday during *salongo* time, I went out in a Land Rover with a friend and little Georgia. Unknown to us, no vehicles were supposed to be on the roads during the period of *salongo*. Not far from our house we rounded a corner and were suddenly confronted by perhaps three thousand people, mostly women, cutting grass along both sides of the road. Immediately they began to shout and to throw rocks, grass, sticks, and dirt. I did not know what they were angry about, but I knew we could be in big trouble if we didn't get out of there quickly. I told the driver to step on it. He "floorboarded" his gas pedal and leaned on the horn. As we sailed through the mob, extending a quarter of a mile down the road, they literally showered us with anything and everything they could find to throw.

When we finally emerged on the other side, we traveled a safe distance and then stopped to assess the damage. One window was shattered. Little Georgia was sitting in the back, very erect and solemn, grass and dirt covering her head and neck. Her lower lip was puckered, and just a hint of tears shone in her eyes, but she was unhurt and had not made a whimper. The incident had no racial motivation—we were sure of that. It was simply that we were fair game for being on the road on a *salongo* day!

4. *Sudden holidays.* We never knew when these would be announced. We might be at work at seven o'clock in the morning, or nine o'clock, or eleven o'clock, and suddenly word would be received that work must stop and everyone go home. Why? Sometimes a reason would be given, but more often no one would know.

One such sudden holiday was declared the week after an army general was killed in a helicopter crash. On that day, we started work as usual. As soon as things were running smoothly, I drove the car down to Secli-Wenji, a village fifteen miles south of Mbandaka. We had left our boat there at a repair shop, and I was anxious to see how the work was progressing.

When I arrived, I noticed that all the workers were sitting out in front talking to one another.

"What's going on?" I asked. "Why aren't you working today?"

"Today has been declared a holiday," one of the men replied.

"A holiday. Why?"

"Because the general got killed in that helicopter crash."

"But that was last week. Why is there a holiday today?"

"We don't know. We just got the word to quit work because the general was killed."

Utterly frustrated, I blurted, "That's ridiculous—stopping work all over the country because a general was killed last week. It is regrettable that anyone is killed in an accident, but is stopping work going to bring him back to life?"

One of the men in the group jumped up and angrily shook his finger at me. "What are you saying?" he shouted. "You are against our revolution!"

"I against your revolution!" I retorted. "No! You and the others who are pleased to sit with folded arms and do nothing are the ones who are against the revolution! What is the slogan of your ruling party? It is PEACE, JUSTICE AND WORK. Friend, I am solidly and fervently for *PEACE*. I believe in *JUSTICE* with all my being. And, Citoyen, I know the value and necessity of *WORK*. I want to work. I want to be at least a small part of bringing a better life to your people through some of my own work. No, you're wrong. I am not against your revolution. I'm for it, if it really means what it says. You are the antirevolutionary."

The other men were all ears, but they weren't saying anything. My accuser, not sure how to respond to this line of reasoning, mumbled again that I was against their revolution and that I had better watch what I said. Then he turned and walked off.

I got in the car and drove back to Mbandaka, frustrated and disgusted, knowing that our two crews at the Block and Sand Project and the construction site were also sitting down with folded arms. We would have to wait until tomorrow to work again.

In spite of these endless interruptions, by August of 1974 we had twelve houses under construction, with a roof on the first one. The committee of the Fund for Humanity decided it was time to choose the initial twenty families. And on Sunday afternoon, August 11, we met with these first families at Bokotola to explain the proposal and to answer their questions.

The meeting was held in Lokesa's house—not quite finished, but it did have a roof—and it was packed with people of all ages. We started with a time of joyous singing. Then Pastor Mpombo explained the rules of the project and its philosophy. After his talk I re-emphasized the idea of the Fund for Humanity and the importance of their participation in the whole effort. There was a great spirit in that gathering. I felt good about the prospects for real sharing and involvement.

Two months later, in October of 1974, Lokesa and his family moved into the first house at Bokotola. By Christmastime four other families were living there in their new homes, and the last houses in the twenty of the first group had been started. The day after Christmas we selected the next group of fifteen families. By March the first twenty houses were completed and we had begun on the next group of fifteen. Nine more families were chosen.

All groups of families after the first set were chosen in advance of actual construction, thus allowing the prospective homeowners time to clear their lots in preparation for the foundation. That was always a beautiful scene. Every afternoon for several weeks after each selection, whole families worked up and down the streets, energetically removing weeds, bushes, and roots. It was exciting to be able to share in their anticipation.

By July of 1975, thirty-five of the families had started making monthly payments into the Fund for Humanity. At that point the Fund was receiving over three hundred Zaires a month from house payments, which immediately went into materials for more houses.

In November we selected the fourth group of families. Thirty-three this time, bringing the total number of families chosen to seventy-seven. By the end of 1975, seventy houses had been started; thirty were completed. Many more waited, partially finished, due to shortages of materials.

One of the biggest obstacles to our work was the constant problem of obtaining building supplies. Since we were constructing concrete block houses, our most important ingredient was cement. With this we poured foundations, made blocks, and built walls. We could be out of almost any other building material and keep going, but without cement we would be stopped.

From the very beginning of the venture I prayed and worked diligently to keep a supply of cement on hand. And in truly amazing ways, in spite of a variety of problems, and even though our consumption was often over fifteen tons a week, we were never out of cement a single day. Several times we were down to less than fifty sacks, but always something would happen to replenish our stock.

Early in the project we were buying cement for $1.60 a bag. We expected the price to increase, so we placed a large order and paid for it in order to be assured of the old price. Four months went by, but no cement came. Then we received a letter informing us that the price had been increased and that we must send an additional ninety cents per bag to get delivery on our order. I was sure this procedure could not possibly be right. We had made a contract; our money had been accepted; delivery had been promised. To be required, four months later, to add thousands of dollars in order to obtain delivery violated the most elementary principles of contract law.

I dispatched Ikete four hundred miles to Kinshasa to consult with a Zairois lawyer. He returned a few days later with the sad news that in Zaire such procedure was indeed legal. The Government had authorized the hike in price and made it retroactive, affecting hundreds of orders the company had allowed to stack up while awaiting the new price. We were forced to fork over the extra money, and we still had to wait four more months before we finally received the order. In the meantime we would have run out of cement, had it not been for the English construction company, which sold us nearly one hundred tons from their stock.

On several other occasions we were on the verge of running out of cement and at the last minute someone would come in with a quantity of it to sell. Once, when we were almost out, we did not have money to buy more. At that point a Portuguese businesswoman in town learned of our plight and volunteered to lend us, interest free, two thousand dollars to buy cement. We became good friends with a Belgian who was directing the construction of a new hotel in Mbandaka, and he, on several occasions, loaned us a total of nearly one hundred tons of cement. The Catholics in Mbandaka often loaned us cement also, as well as other supplies we needed.

One day in early 1976 our work foreman said to me, "Monsieur Fuller, we have been building at Bokotola now for over two years, and we have never once been out of cement. That is a miracle!"

In the early stages of the project when our cement stock was low we would all be nervous, wondering what we could do to get more. But after so many experiences with cement appearing at the needful time from such an unexpected variety of sources, we finally came to believe it always would—and we stopped worrying about it!

We did, however, run out of just about everything else at one time or another. For months there was no tin to be bought in Zaire. Or no glass. No ceiling material. Or no construction steel for the lintels above the doors and windows.

This steel problem was the most critical, because without steel we couldn't build the walls any higher than the top of the doors and windows. Once, when our supply of steel was down to less than enough for two more houses, I was feeling desperate. Then I remembered seeing some steel at an abandoned port just south of Mbandaka. I went out to look. Sure enough, there was a large supply of steel there, all bent up but usable for our purposes. I got in touch with the custodian responsible for that site, and he contacted the main office in Kinshasa. The answer came back the next day: "You can have it all, free of charge!" It was enough for forty houses.

Without tin, we couldn't put on roofs, but we could continue putting up walls. At one point we had the walls built on more than twenty houses that had no roofs. Then a Zairois army general loaned us enough tin to cover six of them. I made a trip to Kinshasa, enlisting the aid of fellow missionaries Bob and Jane Williams and church president Doctor Bokeleale to get us on a priority list at the factory. They were successful in purchasing enough tin to cover another fifteen houses, and they shipped it upriver to us on a private barge.

Without glass, we couldn't finish the windows. As a stopgap measure, we bought a supply of plywood and nailed it over the windows so the families could move in while we waited for the glass.

Shortages of dozens of smaller items caused endless problems. Once we needed a battery for the truck. There were none in Mbandaka, so we ordered one from Kinshasa and had it shipped by Air Zaire. It arrived smashed to pieces. We filed a claim with the airline, but they never paid. Often we needed V-belts for the block-making machine or the conveyor belt, but there weren't any available. Grease—none in town. Oil—it will be available next week. Shovels—we've ordered some; maybe they'll come within a couple of weeks. Nails—yes, we have them, but we don't know the price, so we can't sell them.

Sometimes when we were hunting for something and it wasn't in any of the stores in town, we would put the word out that we wanted to buy such and such an item. Within a day or two, someone would always come walking up to the door with just what we needed. We became suspicious, however, that we might be buying stolen merchandise, so we discussed that possibility with church officials. It was decided that we should buy items from people only if they could produce a formal bill of sale on a printed form or if we had personal knowledge that the material was not stolen. From that time on, when we asked the prospective vendor for proof that the proffered item had been acquired honestly, he would often just walk off.

We simply had to learn to live with these perpetual shortages. We kept the work going with whatever materials we did have, however, and by March 1, 1976, we were able to choose the fifth group of Bokotola families—twenty-three—making a total of one hundred. By the end of the month all of the houses had been started; thirty-five were finished; and the masonry work had been completed on thirty more.

As the building of the houses progressed, we had to develop other aspects of the community as well. Opening up roads was a big frustration. In late February of 1974, the Government took back its bulldozer for use in the interior, and we were obliged to continue the road work by hand. The Government office responsible for roads and streets kept promising help, but it never came.

Another need was for drainage. When Chuck Clark, our volunteer architect, arrived in October of 1974, I gave him the job of creating a system of drainage ditches leading into the large ditch that emptied into the Zaire River. All of this work also had to be done by hand. When the ditch-digging was well under way, I asked Chuck to take over from me the job of laying out new houses on the lots so the foundations could be dug. Also, I asked him to put in the remaining boundary markers. Those tasks together would involve months of work in surveying the lots and placing more than two hundred permanent boundary markers.

Ikete, the projects director of the church, was transferred to our payroll about this time, because practically all the other projects had been closed down. Chuck began to work with him, teaching him how to survey, to place the boundary markers, and to lay out the houses. Ikete was a quick learner and within three months Chuck turned this work completely over to Ikete and was free to begin designing new house models and the community park.

Don Mosley, Boango, the church builder, and I had collaborated on the design of the first group of houses, but since that time the cost of materials had just about doubled. We had to come up with some models that would be cheaper to build, and Chuck soon succeeded in doing this.

We had laid out the housing project reserving a triangular plot of land for a community park. When it was time to develop this area, Chuck again closeted himself in his room. Some time later he emerged with his creation. We took it to church leaders and they were enthusiastic. The plan included a community building with surrounding terraces, and for the children a hollow concrete dome with a connecting runway, a set of parallel walls for climbing, a pyramid of cement blocks, a large sand pit, and a soccer field. He even incorporated one of the giant anthills, capitalizing on children's universal pleasure in sliding down dirt piles. The ants were still in residence, but they stayed deep inside and never bothered the children.

By September of 1975, all the structures in the park had been completed. What a popular place it became! The community building was used daily for the workers' morning worship service. The Government education office asked to use the building each morning, after the worship service, for classes for preschool children; they also requested Linda's help in developing materials for this age group, and before long she was working with 14 schools, involving 40 teachers and 1,600 children. Women's sewing and cooking classes met under her leadership two afternoons a week. In the late afternoon the building was a gathering place for the men, who came after work to lounge and visit. On other occasions it was used for funerals, church meetings, and even as a courtroom for settling community disputes. The play area of the park was literally covered with children every afternoon after school. It was the only facility of its kind in the city, and the children came from miles around to enjoy it.

The women found one inadequacy in the community building. It had open sides and curved benches, with a big worktable at one edge. After lunch, when the women held their sewing and cooking sessions, the afternoon sun blazed down on the worktable, and the wind often blew their projects away. The over-all layout was not conducive to teaching. Something was needed especially for the women.

Again we called on Chuck, and he, in co-operation with

Linda, Helen Weeks (another Disciples missionary who was working with Linda), and the women of the community, designed a structure for the women's *"foyer sociale."* It was an apse, a semi-dome of ferro-cement positioned to shield the women from the afternoon sun, with a big demonstration table and semicircular benches which could double as worktables. Behind the benches was an area for a model garden. Over the benches and the garden area was a trellis covered with huge bamboo trunks. The women were pleased and gratified to have their special place, and in January of 1976 the "foyer" was dedicated with a colorful ceremony of singing, dancing and drumming.

Cindy Miller, another of our American volunteers, had been painting houses since her arrival a few months before. Now she took over the planting of the demonstration garden under the trellis. She also started working with individual families to help them develop gardens on their own lots.

We built a furniture-making shop in Mbomba's back yard, a chicken house in Ikete's back yard, and a small clinic in the back yard of Ilanga, who was a trained nurse at the general hospital in town. All of these enterprises were financed by the Fund for Humanity, and repayment schedules were set up to cover a period of years, along with the monthly house payments.

As soon as there were thirty families living at Bokotola, they organized and elected the customary village chief. They also chose a work foreman for community projects, a community pastor, and an advisory committee of two men and two women.

Quite often, being named to receive a house at Bokotola was an overwhelming emotional experience. One night, after we had chosen a new group of families earlier in the day, a man came to my house to ask if he had been selected. When I told him he had, he was struck totally dumb for several minutes. I really feared that he might collapse. Another man, upon being informed that his family had been chosen, ran to his lot and fell on his knees in prayer. The morning after the selection of one of the masons at the project, I was walking toward the lot where he was laying blocks. When he saw me, he threw down his trowel and came running over. He fell to his knees, grasped my hand tightly between his and repeated over and over: *"Merci! Merci! Merci!"* Still another man told me that when he informed his family they would have a new house at Bokotola, they broke into spontaneous singing and dancing that went on for an hour.

Even being considered for a house could be an overwhelming experience. Before every choice of families, an Investigation Committee was appointed to visit each proposed family's actual living situation. One day Ikete, Larry Stoner and I were doing this investigation. We arrived at a place where nineteen people were living in a two-room mud shack. When the father saw us, he ran and fell on his knees before us, folding his hands in an attitude of prayer. Larry especially was so embarrassed he hardly knew what to do. The man was beside himself. He got up, walked toward the house, came back, returned, and then brought a table to set before us; he continued to wring his hands and mumble incoherently throughout our visit.

The fortunate families were tremendously proud of their new homes. Late one afternoon I was standing on the street in front of the first row of houses with some of the people who had recently moved in. They were in an expansive mood as they chatted and looked out over their new settlement. One man waved his arm in a wide sweep toward the houses and exclaimed, "Look! Do you think the colonialists ever intended to build beautiful houses like these for a group of Niggers? Never! Never! Never!" Everybody cracked up with boisterous laughter. The answer was obvious. Prior to independence, the Belgians had launched a tentative housing program, but the largest homes built were tiny two- and three-room boxes that were much too small for a family. Now the church, with its inadequate resources, was building adequate houses for the people. The contrast made a powerful impact.

By mid-1976, a total of one hundred families had been chosen, and all of their houses had been started. Forty-five were finished, and masonry work was completed on another thirty-five. These eighty families were making house payments, returning to the Fund for Humanity $750 a month. Four hundred people were already living in the community, and new families were moving in nearly every week.

In late 1975 we had returned to the office of the Regional Commissioner to ask for an extension of Bokotola. This time there was no hesitation. "Decide precisely what land you want. Make a map of it, with a description, and we will grant it to you!"

Chuck got busy again, and with Ikete and a crew of workmen he surveyed the adjacent land and laid out lots for forty-eight more houses and a second community park. He put in boundary markers for the outside limits and left the job of staking the intermediate markers with Ikete. When Chuck departed for the States shortly thereafter, he had already stayed three months longer than his intended one year.

As Bokotola took form right in the heart of Mbandaka, the entire city buzzed with interest. Naturally, those families which were selected for new houses were the most excited, but the excitement was by no means limited to them. In the midst of so many problems, so much hopelessness, Bokotola was a blossoming, highly visible sign of hope and progress. The love and concern of Christ's church were clearly evident in this growing community.

8
Partners

IN March of 1974, when we began construction in Bokotola, the building permit was not the only thing we were missing. We did not have enough money to finish even one house! But we did have a promise—from the Plymouth Congregational Church in Plymouth, New Hampshire—of funds sufficient to complete our initial unit. And that's the way we proceeded. We were always broke, but enough money to keep us going always miraculously came in.

One of our earliest and most consistent supporters was the Bethel United Church of Christ in Evansville, Indiana. Jim Prickett, the pastor, was one of the first people to write us after we arrived in Zaire in July of 1973.

In August: "We'll pray for your work in Zaire. Just as God called you to that work, so He is calling us to join the team. Let us know how we can help ..."

In October: "Our Board of Christian Outreach voted to take on Millard Fuller (questionable character!) as a special project beginning January first. We'll conduct a drive to raise two thousand dollars for a house ..."

Before the end of the year, this church had paid for the house, and they kept going after that until they bought a new motorbike for one of our volunteer builders, and then they helped pay for a new dump truck.

Don Mosley, back at Koinonia, was an ardent supporter and fund raiser. In May he went to Evansville to help that church with the campaign for Bokotola. Then he set up a program to gather used eyeglasses to send to us. We had discovered there were *no* eyeglasses available in the entire area of Equator Region, so we decided to ask friends at home for used ones; then sell them at a small price and use the proceeds to build more houses. An appeal was made through the Koinonia mailing list, and over three thousand pairs of eyeglasses were shipped to us in barrels. An additional one thousand pairs came in smaller batches, shipped directly by individuals and churches.

We set up three distribution points in Mbandaka, one in Bolenge, and several more in surrounding villages. In the local prison, we sold eyeglasses for one dollar a pair. Outside, women's eyeglasses were two dollars and men's were two dol-

lars and fifty cents. Thousands of people acquired hitherto
unobtainable eyeglasses, and with our "glasses money" we
built three more houses!

On a busy workday in 1975 the eyeglasses project even
helped us settle another of our constant hassles with the gendarmes. One of our truck drivers was arrested for not wearing
eyeglasses.

"But I don't ever wear eyeglasses. I don't *need* eyeglasses,"
he expostulated.

"We have a new ruling," the gendarme intoned. "From now
on, all drivers of large trucks must wear eyeglasses. It is too
dangerous to drive a big truck without eyeglasses. I will let
you go this time, but if I catch you driving a truck like this
again without eyeglasses, you will have to pay a fine."

The driver came back to our Block and Sand office and
scrambled through the supply of used eyeglasses we had for
sale until he found the weakest pair. He put them on and
continued his work. From that day on, he always wore them to
drive the truck; at other times he wore no eyeglasses at all.

I was constantly sending Don Mosley slides and tapes describing the project. He would make duplicates and mail them
all over the country, thus forging vital links in the fund-raising
chain that kept pulling us along.

The Board of Directors of Koinonia was always supportive.
At one point our resources sank so low that we were in danger
of having to stop work. Don contacted the board members and
got their agreement to borrow fifteen thousand dollars from
the bank for us, until more gifts for the Mbandaka Fund for
Humanity came in.

Perhaps the greatest contribution Don made was in finding
volunteer builders. Vern Preheim, Zaire Director of the Mennonite Central Committee, had already sent Dan Froese to us,
but Dan had to leave in March of 1974. Vern convinced his
headquarters in Akron, Pennsylvania, to sponsor some
builders for the Mbandaka project, but the problem was to
locate the right people. And that is precisely what Don did.

Larry Stoner, a Mennonite volunteer who had been coordi-
nating the construction work at Koinonia for two-and-a-half
years, was approaching the end of his tour there. The more
Don talked to him about the needs and opportunities in Zaire,
the more Larry wanted to get involved. Ken Sauder, another
Mennonite volunteer at Koinonia, also became interested,
along with Joe Kirk, a Quaker who had come to work at
Koinonia after I had spoken at his high school in Smithville,
Ohio. All three of them decided to apply to the Mennonite

Central Committee for sponsorship to Zaire. The Central Committee accepted them all! Larry arrived in September of 1974; Ken came in November of the same year; and Joe reported the following April.

In the meantime, another young man showed up at Koinonia, and Don kept talking to him about Mbandaka. He was Chuck Clark, a native of North Carolina who had recently graduated from the school of architecture at Georgia Tech. He decided he would like to come out and help us for a year. Following six weeks of training and preparation at Koinonia, Chuck rounded up enough cash for his plane ticket out, while we reserved money from the Lilly grant for living expenses and his return fare, and he was on his way. Chuck arrived in October of 1974.

One of our earliest boosters—and one who also played an important part in sending us volunteers —was Raymond Martin of the Eastern Mennonite Board of Missions and Charities. I had gotten to know him when I was director of Koinonia Partners and we were regularly receiving volunteers through his office for work at Koinonia. Soon after I arrived in Zaire, I wrote Raymond about what we were attempting to do. He answered in November of 1973:

> I was very happy to hear what you are doing. The project sounds really interesting. If I can be helpful in any way, I certainly want to. I see you are already in touch with Vern Preheim, and I suppose that anything we would do would be through the Mennonite Central Committee. Perhaps we can supply personnel, and I also want to explore possibilities for financial help ...

Both Raymond and Vern followed through on these needs. In April Vern made a formal request to the Eastern Mennonite Board for a grant to buy a thousand sacks of cement ($3,200); this was soon approved. Later, two more substantial gifts were made by this same group. And in 1976 the Mennonite Central Committee made a direct grant of $5,000 to the project.

An exciting feature of the Fund for Humanity has been the broad ecumenical nature of the groups who have been moved to help. When Don Mosley came out to do the survey work, his trip was paid for by a combination of Methodist, Baptist, and Hutterite churches, and an Assembly of God businessman.

The Wisconsin Baptist Men of the American Baptist Churches conducted a fund drive for Bokotola; as did the Michigan Baptist Men of the Progressive Baptist Church. *Guideposts* Magazine contributed $2,500; so did the Quaker organization "Right Sharing for World Resources." The Reformed Church in America added $2,000. A German organization, "Bread for the World," loaned $5,000 to the Synod of Equator Region, which in turn loaned it to the Fund for Humanity. The Disciples made loans totaling $30,000 and a grant of $10,000. The United Church of Christ Board for World Ministries added a second grant of $5,000 to their first one which had replaced old equipment in the Block and Sand Project. We received substantial gifts from the United Church of Christ in Swampscott, Massachusetts; the Todd Congregational Christian Church in Shawmut, Alabama; the First Christian Church of Wilmington, Delaware; the First Baptist Church of Winston-Salem, North Carolina; and a group of house churches in Kitchener, Ontario, Canada.

The Congregational Church of Laconia, New Hampshire, sent a beautiful memorial. Horace Ballard, a member of the congregation, had been planning to come with his wife to do volunteer work at Bokotola. A few days before they were scheduled to leave the States Horace suddenly died; shortly thereafter the church gave $2,000 to build a house in his memory.

The backbone of our support came from individuals who kept plugging. Without these earnest friends at home, we could never have realized the dream of Bokotola.

Sterling Schallert, a lawyer and American Baptist layman from Wisconsin, who contributed generously, also sought and obtained help from others. Bob Wood, of Westport, Connecticut, who had been part of the group who organized the original Fund for Humanity at Koinonia in 1968, was a perpetual encourager and promoter. He was instrumental in the publication of an article in the April 1975 issue of *Faith at Work* Magazine which precipitated much support for the project and brought us another volunteer, Cindy Miller. Cindy, who joined us in late 1975, was the daughter of Robert Miller, a Presbyterian minister and another of the founding group of Koinonia Partners. Margaret Glocker, of Dayton, Ohio, contributed personally, solicited eyeglasses, persuaded her local Presbyterian church to support us, and instituted a request for a $10,000 grant from the Self-Development of People Fund of the United Presbyterian Church. John Newell, also of Dayton, took a "moonlighting" job in his field of computer programming and sent all these earnings to Zaire.

We were thankful that people who came to visit the project usually went home as enthusiastic fund raisers. The Rev. John and Lucile Compton visited Mbandaka soon after our arrival; upon their return home they were successful in raising nearly $1,000 in their United Christian Church of Cincinnati, Ohio,

for the Fund for Humanity. Pressley Ingram, of Birmingham,
Alabama, came out to see us twice—the first time to visit and
the second time to do volunteer work for a six-week period; he
and his church's men's group became faithful contributors.
Larry Stoner's family visited him on the project in October of
1975; when they returned to their Mennonite church in Lititz,
Pennsylvania, the slides they had taken generated many more
gifts for Bokotola.

Whenever our finances became discouragingly low, Linda or
I would take to the typewriter. Constantly in my mind was
something Clarence Jordan had said to me back when we were
setting up the Fund for Humanity in Georgia: "We've got to
become monumental beggars for God's people in need."

So I made no apologies for begging. I would write a progress report to interested friends concerning the Block and
Sand Project, the housing development, the latest recipients
of wooden legs. I would describe the cramped and crumbling
mud houses, the high cost of living, and the local salaries aver-
aging from twenty to thirty-five dollars a month. I would point
out that the project could make a visible dent in the terrible
needs of this city, in the name of Christ, and that the program
was designed to become self-perpetuating. And then the
catch: our total requirements were going to run over a quarter
of a million dollars ... and we needed *HELP*.

After one such letter we received a prompt response and a
large check from Dorcas Davis, of Charleston, West Virginia,
and more gifts followed. Her partnership with us was a gift
from God, as was the tremendous support, through gifts and
letters and prayers, of a host of other concerned Christians,
many of whom we have never met. Their return addresses
were almost an atlas of the United States, but all their love
came from the same special Source.

These faithful friends included:

Leroy and Venora Ellis and their Episcopal church in Nor-
walk, Conn.
Bill and Joan Clarke in Canton, Ohio.
Ed Carlson in Rockford, Ill.
Judy Evans Vohs in Concord, Calif.
Curtis and Nancy Petrey and their Methodist church, Tupelo,
Miss.
Vic and Diane Scott in Salem, N.J.
Donald and Lena Brady and their Congregational church, Bra-
denton, Fla.
Howard and Pauline Stalker in Middletown, Ohio.
Ralph and Helen Kennedy in Lamar, Ind.
Dr. and Mrs. Warren Proudfoot in Morehead, Ky.

Bob and Penny Clabaugh in Incline Village, Nev.

Lucile Patrick in Delton, Mich.

Dr. and Mrs. Donald Yates in Terre Haute, Ind.

Clem and Ailene Orr in Laconia, N. H.

Mr. and Mrs. Harold James in Toledo, Ohio.

Irving and Julie Harris in Princeton, N. J.

Joanie Collyer in New York, N. Y.

Rosa Page Welch in Denver, Colo.

Bruce Larson in Sanibel, Fla.

Esther Howard in Columbia, Md.

Helen Stephens and her Community church in New Hampton, N.H.

David and Lorraine Cogan in the Bronx, N.Y.

Phil and Bobbie Hoy in Fort Wayne, Ind.

Jim Sweeny, Jr. in Westport, Conn.

Marge Overturf and her Methodist Church, Oconomowoc, Wis.

Lolly Pomeroy in Talahassee, Fla.

John Staton and the First Congregational Christian Church, Kokomo, Ind.

Clyde Tilley, Union University in Jackson, Tenn.

Bob and Frances Field and the South Congregational Church, Granby, Conn.

Dianna Sanchez in San Antonio, Texas.

Lynn and Ginny Coultas in Havana, Fla.

and there were more.

We thanked God for each one of you, partners.

9
Pastor Lokoni

"YEARS ago, when the missionaries came, the first thing they did was build nice houses for themselves. Next, they built nice houses for God. But they didn't help the people build houses."

Pastor Lokoni spoke in rapid French, pointing his finger toward the two visitors for emphasis. Then he pursed his lips tightly, gazed intently at his listeners, and waited for me to translate. As soon as I finished, he squirmed forward in the chair and continued.

"*Oui!* They built houses for themselves and for God, but not for the people. Later they built schools and clinics, and that was good. We needed those things, but we needed houses, too."

Again a pause and a glance indicating that I should explain his words.

"But finally God sent Mr. Fuller to help us with our problem of housing. And he sent the others, too—Chuck, Ken, Joe, Larry and Cindy—everybody was sent by God! Look around you at these new houses. People are living like human beings. This is God's work—to help the poor people with their needs, not only spiritual ones, but human, physical ones. One of our biggest needs in Mbandaka is housing. People are living like animals. They don't have anywhere to live and they don't have the money to build with. Ask anybody. They will tell you that housing is our biggest need, and it's right that the church is helping the people by building the new community of Bokotola here in the center of the city."

The visitors were Bob and Myrna Gemmer from St. Petersburg, Florida, who were on their way to the November 1975 World Council of Churches meeting in Nairobi. We were sitting in the living room of Mbomba's new house in Bokotola. Mbomba was the work foreman at the project and Pastor Lokoni's best friend. He had just finished serving nine of us a delicious dinner of chicken, fish, rice, *pondu* (cooked leaves of the manioc plant), and *kwanga* (boiled roots of the manioc plant, pounded into a mush and rolled into round gummy chunks).

The lantern on the small table in the middle of the room flickered its light on every face as we leaned forward to catch

the words of this snaggle-toothed pastor-philosopher. Larry
Stoner was there also, along with Ken Sauder, Joe Kirk, and
Chuck Clark.

We had come together many times before to share a meal,
often with visitors from America and elsewhere. Pastor
Lokoni and Mbomba always insisted on furnishing a meal and
having a time of discussion with every visitor who came to see
the project. And it was always Pastor Lokoni who held forth.
His buoyant spirit and keen insights were invariably
delightful.

I had first met Pastor Lokoni soon after arriving in Mbandaka in mid-1973. At that time he was pastor to the central
prison and to the hospitals in the city—General Hospital,
Clinic, and TB Hospital. The central treasury of the Disciples
Community paid his salary, since he had no congregation to
support him. He received 16 Zaires a month.

Pastor Lokoni and his wife had no children of their own, but
they had *nine* children of relatives staying with them and
dependent on them. They were living in Nouvelle Cité, a new
section of Mbandaka that just "happened" as people poured in
after independence in 1960. All the houses there, on tiny plots
of land, were made of mud and sticks, with palm-branch roofs.
Lokoni's house was typical of those in the area: collapsing mud
walls, flimsy roof with enough holes to see the stars at night,
damp mud floor. He and his family never had sufficient food,
and of course there was no money for medicine if someone fell
ill. In spite of everything, Lokoni was a man full of joy and
optimism, always thinking of the needs of others.

When he learned that we were planning to build houses for
the poor and develop a new community, he was overcome with
delight. And though he had no position of authority in the
church of Equator Region, he was my strongest supporter
and encourager. He was a pastor to me, full of assurance that
we were about God's work, telling me in countless ways how
the people were hurting and that a housing program would be
striking at the very heart of their needs.

He was a pastor and friend to those who came to help us in
the work as well. When Dan Froese arrived to do a short tour
of service with us at the very beginning of Bokotola, it was
Pastor Lokoni who taught him the language, introduced him
to people around town, and found workers as he needed them.
A month later, when Don Mosley arrived to survey the land
for the new houses, again it was Pastor Lokoni who was there
to make him feel welcome and encourage him.

At the end of Don's time in Mbandaka, Pastor Lokoni put on
a big feast for him at his little shack. It was a bright, clear
night, and streams of moonlight poured in on us as we ate and

visited together through an unforgettable evening. After the meal, Pastor had us sit around in a tight circle so that he could talk to Don. His first plea was for him to stay with us.

"We need you," he said. "There are others back in America who can do your work there. You stay here and help us with the big job we have ahead."

Don replied that he must go back, but that he wouldn't forget us, that he would always be with us in spirit, and that he would do all he could to help the project by seeking funds and builders to come and work with us.

And in the months ahead, as Don consistently found sources of financial support for us back in the States, and as he recruited volunteer builders to come out to Bokotola, Pastor Lokoni often exclaimed in delight, "Mr. Mosley *is* with us, just as he promised!"

Although Pastor Lokoni was a rather small man, he didn't give that impression when you first met him. It was only after studying his physique that you noticed he was short and had small hands and feet. His very black face was round and a little puffy, with double sets of hairline tribal marks, perpendicular to each other, at either side of his eyes.

When Pastor Lokoni laughed, you saw his four snaggle-teeth; when he was serious, he appeared completely toothless and his speech contained a slight lisp. While he spoke, he looked you straight in the face, with eyes of compassion and feeling, and he talked with his whole body—particularly his hands were in constant motion. He was an intent, affirming listener when others talked to him.

When Pastor Lokoni read the Bible at worship services, it was in a loud monotone, but his preaching was animated and attention-grabbing, and people always listened raptly. Frequently he translated my French into Lingala when I spoke in the prison or at churches in the area. I never had to prepare much when he translated for me. I could say three sentences and he would get carried away and expand it into a ten-minute talk.

Pastor Lokoni was also one of the two members, with Mbomba, of our unofficial welcoming committee for all guests who came to see us and to visit the project. He wanted to make them comfortable, to talk with them about their community and church, and to make sure they understood clearly the need for a project like Bokotola in Mbandaka, in hopes they would return and enlist the help of others. He organized tours of Mbandaka, introducing visitors to families and taking them into homes to see the living conditions of the people.

In February 1974, the Rev. and Mrs. Charles Trent, of Winfield, Kansas, came to see us. Charles is a retired American

Baptist minister, and we had met at Koinonia Farm in Georgia a few years earlier. During their three-day stay in Mbandaka they spent a lot of time with Pastor Lokoni, going with him to the prison and having a meal in his little shack. They were deeply impressed. Just before leaving the country, they bought a bicycle for him in Kinshasa, the capital of Zaire, and sent it to Mbandaka by a church leader. The letter he wrote in response could scarcely convey his excitement and pleasure:

When I saw the bicycle you sent, I was emotional. Thank you *very* much. And I say thanks to God, too, who has shown me the road for saving his slave. I was having much difficulty in coming and going each day by foot ...

Pastor Lokoni continued to correspond faithfully with his American friends, and, in June, Charles Trent informed me that he and his wife had decided to make a gift of one-half the cost of a new house for Pastor Lokoni and his family in Bokotola. Overwhelmed, Pastor Lokoni sent another excited thank you to Kansas:

My joy is great in writing you this letter. In the name of Jesus Christ, all the family as well as myself, give you a warm handshake!
Rev. Pastor, I never had the hopes of having one day a good and beautiful house. But as God has informed you about my state of poverty and suffering, now I rejoice, for I hope to live in a house suitable for my family. They have already started the work on my house. The house where I live remains as always in a disgusting state, when it rains I suffer. But Mr. Fuller told me they are going to finish my house fast ...

I enclosed a letter of my own with that of Pastor Lokoni:

As you can see, you have brought great joy to this fine family. When I shared the news with Pastor Lokoni about your gift, he slowly folded his hands in front of him in an attitude of prayer, and an incredibly wide smile spread across his face. "Praise God, praise God," he said. "God is with us!" He selected the lot he likes on the building site, and we went to work immediately. Already the foundation is dug and part of it is poured. Before you get this letter, the walls will be going up. Pastor Lokoni is working every day too, as much as his schedule permits. He is truly excited, and totally happy, I can assure you of that! I will be sending you pictures as the work progresses. I have promised him that we will expedite the work as much as possible, and I'm hoping to have him in the house by Christmas ...

In August, Pastor Lokoni was named "project pastor" by church leaders. He continued at the prison, but his work at the hospitals was taken over by another pastor. In this new capacity, Pastor Lokoni worked at the construction site each day. He organized the morning worship services for the workers, visited any who were sick, including their family members, counseled the men concerning their personal problems ... and started learning to lay blocks!

Some other pastors around town criticized him, saying it was not dignified for a pastor to work with his hands or to be seen with dirty hands and clothes. He didn't like this criticism, but he was not deterred. Pastor Lokoni saw himself as a servant, and no work was beneath him.

Another pastor in town had been assigned a new house in the community and was very anxious to move in, but his toilet had not been completed. The work foreman, Mbomba, suggested that he move in and simply use the toilet of a neighbor until his own was finished. The pastor firmly rejected that suggestion, saying it wouldn't be proper for a pastor to use a layman's toilet. When Mbomba told me this, I said, "But Pastor Lokoni uses your toilet!" (He was so anxious to leave his miserable shack that he had moved into his house when only the kitchen had been finished—no floor, no doors, no windows, no toilet.)

Mbomba broke out in a wide smile. "But that's different. Pastor Lokoni *loves* laymen!"

This was certainly true. Pastor Lokoni was always sensitive to the needs of those around him. Once, when we were obliged to reduce our work force because of a shortage of funds, I asked Pastor Lokoni and Mbomba to give me their thoughts on who should be fired. Mbomba quickly held his hand in front of my face and asked me not to talk about this in Pastor Lokoni's presence.

"Why?" I responded, quite surprised.

I looked over at Lokoni. He was staring down at his feet.

Mbomba replied for him. "It hurts him too much. He knows the men and their families will suffer. He would rather not be a part of this discussion."

Pastor Lokoni loved our volunteers, too. As soon as the fellows started arriving in late 1974 he began a campaign to get them to live with him. Eventually two moved in: first Ken Sauder, our Mennonite builder from Mt. Joy, Pennsylvania, and then Chuck Clark, our architect from Georgia. Pastor Lokoni called them"*Mes enfants* [my children]," and made them feel right at home. Ken stayed a few months, then moved in with another Bokotola family. Chuck lived with the Lokonis for nearly a year.

When Chuck's tour of service ended, the community organized a program of appreciation for him in the community building, and Pastor Lokoni was one of the principal speakers. He told how much it had meant to him and his family to have Chuck there. "He was just like a member of the family," he said. "He ate the same food we ate, he lived right in the house with us, he took his bath out back just like we do and he went to the same toilet we use. *Il était mon enfant!* [He was my child!]"

Everyone roared with laughter, clapping and nodding in enthusiastic affirmation.

After Chuck left, Pastor Lokoni began urging Cindy Miller to live with them. She had moved in with us when she had first arrived in Mbandaka, but soon after Chuck returned to the States she went to live with Pastor Lokoni and his family. He had his first fair-haired daughter, and he was enormously pleased.

In the meantime, Bokotola was under way. On October 20, 1974, I wrote to the Trents:

We moved the first family in this week! I wanted to share this good news with you immediately. We now have the roofs on eight of the houses. Fifteen are under construction. The second family will move in next week and the third the following week. Pastor Lokoni's house is going up, too—within the next two weeks we will start putting on his roof. He will definitely be in his house before Christmas ...

On November 26 I was able to write the Trents:

Pastor Lokoni will move into his new house tomorrow. He is ecstatic! His is the fifth house to be occupied.

And it was none too soon—his old house was just about to fall down. Every day he pitched in alongside the other workmen, laboring steadily to complete the building. By Christmas he had a finished house, and the whole family joyfully moved in. Meanwhile, as project pastor, prison pastor and budding block mason, his salary had doubled.

Life for Pastor Lokoni was looking up—and the dream of Bokotola was becoming a reality.

10
Mbomba

I WAS standing in the entrance of the road we were building into Bokotola. The young man standing before me had been coming daily for several weeks to ask for work. I had always told him to wait, wait, *wait*. We were having trouble getting the road built up enough to take a truck laden with building materials, and we still did not have that elusive building permit.

The young man, Mbomba by name, had first approached Dan Froese for a job. Dan had hired him temporarily to help in constructing two dozen concrete boundary markers for the first lots cleared by the bulldozer. We both had been favorably impressed with his speed and efficiency in that job. But when he finished, we were still not ready to hire him, or anyone else, on a permanent basis.

"I'm sorry, we still can't hire you. Maybe you had better look for a job elsewhere. We just don't know when we'll be able to start."

Mbomba replied firmly, "I have my hope in this project. I am going to wait."

And he waited ... and waited. By February 21, 1974, the road over the bog had been filled in enough to sustain our dump truck, and my patience with the building officials had been exhausted. We hired Mbomba and began digging the following day.

Mbomba was perhaps 5 feet 9 inches tall, stocky but not fat, with large strong hands and arms, an open face that readily broke into a wide smile, and a mouth filled with pearly white teeth. He spoke French, but not very well. Actually he had little formal education, but he had lots of intelligence and personality, combined with a drive that was most unusual among the Zairois. Mbomba was to become a significant factor in the success of Bokotola.

It soon became clear that "by chance" the very first man we had hired was the natural leader we needed as a foreman, or "*capita*," to direct our growing work force. Mbomba was anxious to learn. He insisted that I teach him all I knew about laying-off houses, pouring foundations, building walls. He constantly pushed to go faster. If I said we should complete a foundation in three days, he wanted to do it in two. When we could do it in two, he wanted to cut it to one. He was never absent or late, and his attitude was always positive. I was more and more amazed at what an exceptional man we had hired.

Many times I thought—and remarked to others—that surely God had sent us this seemingly ordinary fellow who turned out to be just the foreman we needed. As a result, working with Mbomba and sharing life with him became one of my greatest joys during our stay in Zaire.

After we had been building for several months, Mbomba suggested that we have a session every Saturday afternoon to discuss the progress of the past week and to plan for the coming week. Until that time we had been doing this on the run from day to day. By that time Pastor Lokoni was working in the project, and Mbomba suggested that he should come too.

Our Saturday afternoon get-togethers soon turned into great times, not only for organizing the work, but for rich fellowship. Mbomba or Lokoni would start the meetings with a song or two; then we would pray and ask God to be in our midst and guide our thoughts. Finally would come the evaluating and the planning. Mbomba was never quite satisfied with what we had accomplished, and he would tell me about the mentality of the Zairois, explaining that we had to do certain things to facilitate the work. "We know our brothers," he would say, "so we've got to do it this way."

At one point there was a lot of dissension among the workmen. Construction slowed down and little was accomplished. At the next Saturday meeting Mbomba told me he had found the trouble. It was Kobongo.

"If we fire Kobongo our problem will end. He is creating all the problems. He is not happy with me as *capita*, so he is getting the men to work against me."

I didn't want to believe that. Kobongo was an agreeable fellow and a very capable carpenter; I had hired him as soon as we finished the masonry work on the first house and were ready to put on the roof. I told Mbomba I would talk to Kobongo. I preferred to solve the problem in some way other than by dismissing him.

When I brought up the subject with Kobongo, he strongly denied that he was working against Mbomba, and insisted that he was completely happy with Mbomba's leadership. I pointed out to him that we had a problem with workmen who were not following Mbomba's instructions, and I needed his help in changing the situation. I told him I knew the men looked up to him and that he was in a crucial position to form attitudes. He assured me he would do all he could to work positively with Mbomba and to help things go smoothly.

But things still didn't go smoothly. This matter became the topic of Saturday meetings for several weeks. Mbomba kept saying that we must fire Kobongo in order to solve the problem. I didn't want to accept that, and I met numerous times with Kobongo in an effort to avoid that step.

Finally I saw no other way out, so we prepared his dismissal papers. I went with Mbomba and Ikete to inform Kobongo that he was being fired. When we told him, he didn't become emotional, but in a quiet voice he poured out a stream of venom against Mbomba. He said he was older and didn't understand why a young man like Mbomba should be the boss. He reminded us he had a degree from technical school as well as much more experience. He should have been made foreman. On and on he talked. I understood his true feelings for the first time, and I knew we had made the right decision. After Kobongo's dismissal, there was a total change in attitude among the workmen, and we never again had a similar problem.

A few weeks later we had a problem of a quite different sort. I was riding up to the work site on my motorbike when Mbomba hurried out to greet me. *"Bonjour, Patron.* We've got a big problem. Come over here so we can discuss it privately."

I kicked down the stand on the bike and followed Mbomba a short distance to the first vacant lot. Ikete came over with us. Together they began to unfold a fascinating story.

A few days earlier, they said, Akwamenga, one of the masons, had left two Zaires in the pocket of his work pants while he washed up after work, and during that brief few minutes someone had taken the money. He had been very upset. The following day Akwamenga returned to the job and announced that he knew who had stolen his money, that it was Mputu, his boy mason. (Each mason had a helper who mixed cement and brought blocks to him.) He knew this because he had gone to the cemetery and got a red flower from a white man's grave. Then he had gotten some tail feathers from a parrot. He slept with the tail feathers and the flower, and during his sleep he had a dream in which it was revealed to him that Mputu was the thief.

The announcement created great alarm among the workmen. It was decided to get the customary "judge" to hear the matter and decide what must be done. This old man came and, after hearing the case, announced that the dream was not sufficient proof of the guilt of Mputu. Akwamenga had no right to make such an accusation against Mputu without proof. Furthermore, Akwamenga should pay damages to Mputu because he had defamed his character by calling him a thief. To set the amount of these damages, the case should go to the "tribunal" (the big court) and be heard there.

"Now," Mbomba said, "there are two problems. First, what should be done about the question of damages? Second, none of the other workmen will work with Akwamenga. Mputu has refused to work with him any more and all of the other boy masons have also refused. They think he has evil powers. They are afraid of him." Before I could reply, Mbomba stated flatly, "We've got to fire him. There is no other solution."

"Wait a minute," I said, "not so fast. First of all, I can understand why Akwamenga would be very upset about his money being stolen. I've had many things stolen out here, and it makes me mad. You feel anger and frustration and you want to lash out at someone. I can understand trying to find out who was the guilty one ... even to the point of doing something dramatic and drastic. But, first, let's take the question of damages. Isn't Mputu related to Pastor Lokoni?"

"Yes."

"Call Pastor Lokoni over here." He was laying blocks at the house on the adjacent lot with the other masons.

"Pastor," I started when he arrived, "is Mputu a Christian?"

"I don't know. I'll ask him." He turned around and called to Mputu. "Mputu, come here." He stepped down from the side of the anthill where we were talking, and after a brief exchange with Mputu, he walked back to us. "No, he hasn't been baptized."

"Well," I said, "since he isn't a Christian he can just go to the tribunal and try to get as much damages as he can. Perhaps the question of forgiveness is not relevant to him as a non-Christian."

"No," Pastor Lokoni spoke up strongly. "That boy will take my advice, and I don't want him going into court asking for damages. We can forget the question of damages."

"Are you sure?"

"Absolutely. Mputu got his job because of me, and he'll do what I say. Forget the problem of damages."

"Well, then, we've got the problem that no one will work with Akwamenga. I can't agree to fire him without trying to find some better solution. First of all, I'd like to know if Akwamenga is a Christian. Do you know?"

"Yes, he is Catholic."

"Call Akwamenga over here. Let's talk to him and see how he feels about this whole matter."

Akwamenga was working on the adjacent lot with the other

masons, although I noticed he was isolated. No one was coming near him or talking to him, and he was working alone with a solemn look on his face.

"Akwamenga, come here," Pastor Lokoni called.

When Akwamenga was facing us, I asked him if he was a Christian.

"Yes," he answered. "I am a Christian, a practicing Christian."

"Well," I responded, "if you are a Christian, why are you sleeping with flowers and parrot feathers? What has that got to do with being a Christian?"

"Oh, *Patron*, that has nothing to do with being a Christian. All that is nothing."

"Well, if it is nothing, why did you do it?"

"*Patron*, you know the Zairois. But that is nothing. I wanted to get my money back."

"Akwamenga, where are those parrot feathers?"

"They are here in my pocket."

"In your pocket? If they are nothing, why are you carrying them around in your pocket?"

"Oh, I don't know, *Patron*."

"Show them to me."

He pulled out an old ragged billfold, opened it, and carefully removed three tattered red parrot feathers. By this time, the workmen had their eyes glued on us. And Bassanga, the owner of the lot, who was there digging roots and cutting down weeds, had his eyes on us as well.

"Akwamenga, if those feathers mean nothing to you, would you be willing to throw them away?"

In response to that question he dramatically threw the feathers to the ground at his feet. Immediately the whole area exploded into bedlam. It was as if he had opened a cage of cobras. Pastor Lokoni and Mbomba were beside themselves with excitement and were jumping around. The workmen were in a state of extreme agitation. Most upset of all was the owner of the lot who came running at full speed and yelled into the face of Akwamenga, "Get those feathers off my lot! Get those feathers up! Now! Now!"

Akwamenga's normal brown color was pale with fright. He bent over and scooped up the feathers, but he missed one. "You missed one! You missed one! Get it! Get it!" yelled the lot's owner.

Akwamenga hesitated. Bassanga grabbed a big leaf lying near by and with a little stick raked the remaining feather onto it. Then, running wildly, he took off for the back side of the lot, crashing into the bushes as he ran. Minutes later he emerged, pale and shaken. He staggered toward us. When he was a few feet away, he suddenly grabbed his head and started screaming. Huge sweat beads popped out on his forehead. He bent over as if in mortal pain, yelling. "Something's got me! That man has put an evil spell on me! Get him! Get him!"

He stumbled toward the road. In the middle of the road, he continued to scream and yell. "I am dying! I am dying! He is killing me! He is killing me!"

I didn't know what to do. I thought, too, that he might die. All of us stood transfixed, gazing at this writhing, screaming man.

Eventually Bassanga's yelling subsided. He stood bent over, still holding his head, heaving and moaning. Slowly his breathing returned to normal and the sighs and moans ceased. For a period of perhaps five minutes time seemed to stand still. No one moved.

Then I walked over to the man. "Are you all right now?"

He slowly turned his eyes up to me and nodded his head. "Yes, it seems to have passed. But something had my head. I almost died."

"Come on back over here and let's talk about it."

We walked back over to the hill where Mbomba, Ikete and Pastor Lokoni were waiting. Time began to move again. As we started talking, the men slowly went back to work.

"I cannot live on this lot." Bassanga was sadly shaking his head. "This man has put a spell on my lot. I can't live here."

"Are you a Christian?" I asked him.

"Yes, you know I am a Christian, a member of the same Church as Mbomba." I did in fact know that. I knew the man well. He was secretary of his small congregation, and I had seen him in church numerous times.

"If you are a Christian, Bassanga, why are you so afraid of some parrot feathers?"

Mbomba answered for him. "*Patron*, we are all Christians, but we are Zairois. This is in us. It comes from our past, and we can't just shake it off like that. We don't believe in our heads, but deep down inside us we still believe. It has a powerful hold on us."

"Yes," Bassanga added. "We don't think those feathers have power in them, but we are afraid just the same that maybe they do. I am afraid. And I do know that something had my head a few minutes ago and I thought I was going to die."

I turned to Akwamenga. "Friend, would you be willing to stand up in front of all the workmen and apologize to Mputu and say that the flower and those feathers meant nothing and you only told that story in an attempt to get your money back?"

"Yes, *Patron*, I'll do that."

"Okay. Go back to work. We are going to decide now what to do."

"*Patron*, we've got to fire him." Mbomba was adamant. "If we don't fire him, we are going to have lots of problems. This matter is very serious. Nobody will work with him. And if something happens to Mputu or any of the other workmen, they are going to blame Akwamenga. They will say that he put an evil spell on them, and he will be blamed for any sickness or death that occurs here."

"I can't accept that," I said. "As a Christian I can't be a party to punishing a man because of someone's unreasonable superstition. I want to talk to the men."

By this time, it was nearly three o'clock, and the men were getting ready to quit for the day. I told Mbomba to call them over to the community building for a meeting. And I wanted Bassanga to come, too.

When everyone had gathered, I told them that I regretted the incident, but now we needed to think about the future. I told them that when someone did something against another person, and later asked forgiveness, there were only two things one could do: 1) forgive him, or 2) refuse to forgive and continue to harbor a grudge. For a Christian, I said, it is clear in the Bible that the first possibility is the only real one. But even for the non-Christian, this option makes more sense.

I asked Akwamenga if he was sorry, and if he wanted Mputu to forgive him. In a loud voice, he replied that he was indeed sorry, and he humbly asked Mputu and the others to forgive him.

"You have heard his words," I said. "You can do one of two things: You can believe him and forgive him or refuse to believe him and keep him as an enemy. Which choice makes more sense?

"We must work together. We are here to build not only houses but also a spirit of brotherhood and helpfulness. You have a beautiful country, one of the most beautiful in all of Africa, but if the people in it are full of suspicion, fear, and hatred toward one another, you don't have a beautiful country. All of us are brothers and should live like that. Now let's forget the episode and get on with our work."

Then I looked at Akwamenga and said, "I've got some advice for you, too. You've thrown away the feathers. Don't go looking for any more—and don't ever be caught sleeping with parrot feathers again." Everyone laughed at this and the meeting broke up.

The matter was ended. There was not another word about firing Akwamenga, and we never had any problem with the men not wanting to work with him. Bassanga's house was built. A few months later he and his family moved in, amidst feasting and rejoicing.

As soon as we had three workmen at Bokotola, Mbomba organized a morning worship service. At first it was simply hymn singing and a prayer, but when Pastor Lokoni came a few months later he always gave a meditation or had someone else give one.

Mbomba considered these devotional periods very important. But when our work force grew to over thirty men, some of them non-Christians, there were objections to the service. Mbomba was upset about this.

"We are working in a church-sponsored Project," he insisted, "and the men should gladly join in the full program of the Project, including the service of worshipping God at the beginning of each day."

This problem was the topic of discussion at several Saturday afternoon sessions. Finally we decided to start the worship service at 6:45 A.M. —fifteen minutes *before* work time. Everyone would be invited to attend, but no one would be obligated to come. The roll would be called after the service, and not before, as had been done in the past. On Monday Mbomba would explain the new policy and put it into practice immediately.

The following Saturday, Mbomba was the first to speak in the meeting. "All the men are coming to the morning services just as before, and those who objected to them are usually the first ones to arrive!"

As the months went on, the workmen kept coming. There were rarely absences. All the men participated freely and fully in these times of worship, which had become an important part of the Bokotola project.

Sometimes after the services I would take a few minutes to talk about problems which had arisen. One topic which I frequently felt the need to discuss was the workers' attitude toward the Project itself.

In Zaire a white person is called a *"mundele,"* and the prevailing conviction is that the white man has all the money, owns everything, and knows how to do anything. It is believed that if a *mundele* is the head of an enterprise, it will run smoothly, whereas if a Zairois takes over, it will surely fail.

Among the ordinary everyday Zairois there is a deep-seated inferiority complex. We would often hear questions like: *"Patron*, if God is the God of the blacks and whites, why did He prefer the whites so much, giving them the brains and money, while leaving us so ignorant and poor?"

Or: *"Patron,* is it true that men have gone to the moon?"

"Yes, it is true."

"I'm sure it was white men who went. No black would be intelligent enough to do something like that."

There is also a widespread feeling of nonparticipation in any enterprise of which the Zairois are a part. The workers feel they work *for* the Establishment, not *with* it. The idea of contributing to the well-being of the company or Project, or government office, in order to improve it, and beyond that to improve the city and the nation is almost nonexistent.

Frequently I would be asked, "How is your project going?" And workers at Bokotola would say things like, "Your men unloading sand would like to know what time it is." This attitude of working for me and for *my* Project meant that they felt no real stake in the undertaking. Hence their only concern was to get their salary with the least possible expenditure of energy.

Men would be absent from work for any reason, since their hearts were not really in it. If a child was sick, the father would take it to the hospital instead of sending it with the mother. If a worker's wife was sick, he would stay home. If a relative died, no matter how distant, the worker would not show up. If it was raining, or even if there were clouds in the sky, he might not come.

Of course these attitudes were not shared by everyone. Neither were they shared to the same degree by all. Pastor Bolongwa, for example, the director at the Block and Sand Project, was a man deeply committed to the church and to the Project. Like Mbomba, he worked after hours nearly every day and never asked for a penny in overtime pay. And there were a few others, but the majority shared the attitude of noninvolvement.

This attitude prevailed right up to our departure, but I feel we made significant inroads into it and into some of the others. Time and again I talked to the men about their relationship to the Project, and about the necessity of thinking of it as *their* Project. I pointed out to them that the undertaking was not mine, and that I had only come for a period of time to help them develop something that would be a positive force in the church and in their city. My role was not, I emphasized, to take over the enterprise and make it my own.

I often described the impact the Block and Sand Project and the construction venture were having on the city and the entire area, trying to instill in them pride in being part of the effort. I reminded them they were a free people now, independent of the Belgians, and that it was up to them to make something of their country. And I talked about their feeling of inferiority.

"God," I said, "is the creator of us all. For a multitude of reasons, men find themselves in different situations in life. I don't entirely understand why my country is developed and rich and yours is underdeveloped and poor. But I do understand and accept God's universal love. All men are equally important to God; there are no favorite children in His eyes. Knowing that, any one of us can, and should, stand tall and confident. We should never feel inferior—to do so is to criticize God's handiwork."

Frequently I would emphasize the freedom that God gives us after He creates us.

"What we do with the gift of our lives is up to us. We can squander the talents God has provided or we can develop and use them fully. By the same token, we can use our talents only for ourselves or we can use them for God. A self-centered life is a self-destroying life. To the extent that we live outward-directed lives, to that extent we blossom into the beautiful individuals and society that God intended us to become."

Finally I talked about the country.

"Zaire is one of the most beautiful countries in the world. God has blessed you with great riches—majestic rivers, lush forests, tropical flowers, birds and animals, rich farmlands. What are you going to do with all this?

"In the midst of so much beauty and latent wealth, you have thousands of people hungry, sick, and dying; children ignorant for lack of adequate schools; miserable shacks for houses; insufficient transportation; no jobs. The *mundeles* can come and help, and I hope I can persuade more to come, for the task is enormous. But we must work together to get the job done. You must take the lead in changing the undesirable situation in this land. You must work in a spirit of Christian cooperation to accomplish the gigantic task ahead."

Toward the end of our tour, after another of my postdevotional talks, Bombeto, one of the Block and Sand workers, raised his hand.

"Monsieur Fuller, we want to thank you for teaching us about our work and how we ought to think about it. You are the first *mundele* who has ever talked to us like that. We are beginning to understand what you are trying to say, and we want to thank you."

After the men had left for their jobs that morning, Pastor Bolongwa elaborated on Bombeto's comments.

"Yes," he said. "Bombeto is right. You are the first person ever to talk to us in this way. In the past, men in this country worked out of two motivations: fear and absolute necessity.

They were deathly afraid of the *mundele*, and they felt no interest in the company they worked for. They continued only because they had to have food for their families. But now you are showing the men that things are different and that they should get rid of old attitudes. I think they really are beginning to understand."

If this understanding continues to grow, the example and leadership of Mbomba will have been a major contributing factor. His intense concern for the welfare of the Project, combined with the strength of his personal faith, provided a daily witness to everyone involved with Bokotola.

Not long after Mbomba started work at the Project, he invited me to speak at his church, the smallest and poorest parish in Mbandaka. When we arrived that Sunday morning, a host of smiling people were there to greet us, standing in front of some concrete block walls about five feet high. Poles were stuck into the ground inside the walls. Attached to these poles were others that formed an arch over the top, and these were covered with palm branches. Inside, on a mud floor, there were two rows of logs, separated by a narrow aisle leading up to the front of the "structure." This was the Besenge Church.

Although obviously and painfully poor, the people were joyous and enthusiastic. They crowded in until there was no more room. Others stood in the doorway or peered over the walls. Mbomba had his own singing group which contributed several special songs.

When I stood to speak, my head was in the palm branches. I had to move around until I found a convenient hole into which I could fit my head. Then, looking out through the branches, I delivered my message to the people.

After the service, we were led down a long narrow path to Mbomba's house, where a big meal had been prepared for us. Linda, Faith, and Georgia were with me. The pastor of the church was also there, along with Pastor Lokoni. The house was a classic scene of poverty. The walls were made of mud, the roof of palm branches. To one side of the house was a little open-sided shelter, covered with more palm branches. This was the kitchen, where the women were busily preparing the food. Everything looked old and ready to collapse. The lot was so low and damp that I asked Mbomba about it.

"Yes," he said. "That is a problem for us. When we have lots of rain, water gets up into the house. We have to stay with friends until the water recedes."

In spite of the poverty, the house and lot were clean. We could see that there was a strong sense of pride and dignity in that family, even though they were very poor. We were invited inside. The largest room in the house had been prepared for us, with a sitting arrangement to one side and a table covered with a colorful cloth on the other side. Mbomba came in with his singing group and serenaded us again. Another group followed with more songs. Finally the meal was ready. We were served elephant meat, chicken, fish, *kwanga*, *pondu* and rice. The dessert was a sweetened mixture of banana, pineapple and papaya slices. Everything was good and we ate until we were stuffed.

After the meal, we were again invited to sit in the "living room" area of the room. The food dishes were being hastily carried outside to feed the women and children, who had been waiting for us to finish. (Traditionally, children and women do not eat at the table, but before we left Zaire, Mbomba's wife and the wife of Pastor Lokoni were sitting with us when we ate together. At one meal at Lokoni's house even the children made it!)

Several leading men of the church entered and we were now ready to start our *"causerie* (discussion)." Pastor Lokoni was the spokesman, since the local pastor did not speak French. They wanted to know whether they could obtain assistance in finishing their church. I had seen the pitiful condition it was in, and they were too poor to buy the materials to complete it. Could I help?

I told them to raise the money for the cement, and that I would then send over enough blocks from the Block and Sand Project to finish the walls. Concerning the roof, benches, door, table, chairs, however, I couldn't make any definite promises. They were happy about my proposition to furnish the blocks and agreed that their people could acquire enough money to buy the cement. The discussion ended on that positive note, and we left for home.

In the weeks to come, the people did raise enough money for the cement. I sent over the blocks as I had promised, and Mbomba coordinated the work of finishing the building of the walls.

In the meantime, we had a visitor, Mrs. Mary Ann Williams, from Lake Worth, Florida. She was invited to the Besenge Church and the people asked her to help. She promised to bring the need before her home church, the Union Congregational Church of West Palm Beach, Florida. A couple of months later, we received the good news that the church had voted to pay for a roof for the Besenge Church. When the money was transferred out, we bought the tin and wood and headed for the church.

This was in October of 1974, just a few days after Chuck Clark had arrived. Chuck, Larry, Mbomba, and I took the materials to the church at noon on a Saturday. The pastor, by prearrangement, was already there with some men of the congregation. We had decided to blitz the job and finish it in the same afternoon. We worked at a fever pitch: sawing, nailing, cutting tin, running here and there. The longer we worked the more people came to watch. By twilight, a large crowd had gathered. We were working faster than ever in trying to finish before sundown.

Finally the last piece of tin was handed up to Mbomba. He put it into place and fastened it firmly. When the last nail was driven, he stood up and waved his arms in the air, and the people cheered and clapped ecstatically. Then the pastor threw a song book up to him. He stood there on the cap of the roof and for the next fifteen minutes, as the sun slowly sank out of sight behind him, he led us in singing hymns. It was a magic time.

(Later, the same Union Congregational Church in West Palm Beach donated money for benches, chairs, and a table. Mbomba made them in his new woodworking shop, and they were dedicated in a special service.)

In August, Mbomba was chosen to have a house at Bokotola, and two months later, even though it was not completely finished, he moved in. This was a Saturday afternoon, after the regular workday had ended at noon. He had arranged to borrow the dump truck for moving his furniture. I came home for lunch as he was leaving with the driver to get his things. After lunch I rode back over there to find that he had just finished unloading his family's meager belongings, dumping them in the living room of the new house.

Amid all these disorganized possessions sat Mbomba in a circle with about a dozen friends. Everyone was holding an open Bible, singing and praising God, giving thanks for the gift of a new home. In the hustle and bustle and excitement of moving, Mbomba had arranged a service of dedication for his new house. His pastor was there to give a meditation for the occasion. I slipped in quietly and shared this time of overwhelming joy.

When the pastor finished his talk, everyone rose and filled the house with joyful songs of praise to God. Tears came to my eyes. It was a high moment of religious truth for me. Here was a man of faith, so poor that he had only three or four pieces of furniture (one bed for six people) for a very simple new house. It had no running water or electricity, and an outdoor toilet and kitchen; yet he was putting first things first by praising God even before arranging things in the rooms. I wondered how many families in America or Europe arrange a service of thanksgiving to dedicate a new house. Many of our African Christian friends lack the material things of this world, but they have much to teach our affluent Christian world about the true values in Christian life!

A few weeks after Mbomba moved into his new house, his wife went into the interior to visit some of her relatives. At the same time, I had a trip to Kinshasa to see about buying some more building materials. When I returned to Mbandaka, the first news I heard was that one of Mbomba's children had died.

"One of his children died? Which one?" (He had three children.)

"It was the little girl. Her mother had taken her along on the trip. She died in the interior."

I was talking to Pastor Lokoni. "Where is Mbomba now?"

"He is resting. He was up all night singing and praying with a group of us."

"But how is he? How is he taking this death?"

A big smile came across the face of Lokoni. "Oh, he's all right. He's a Christian!"

And it was true. Mbomba had a faith in God that enabled him to know that everything is ultimately right with those who put their trust in Him.

One day Mbomba and Pastor Lokoni came to me with a proposition.

"Monsieur Fuller," began Mbomba, "we have seen how, over these past months, our Christian friends in America have sent money to help us build Bokotola. We are happy about that. But we want to give, too. Unfortunately, we don't have any money, but we have an idea as to how we can contribute to the project."

Pastor Lokoni continued. "Yes, we have an idea if you are in agreement. Do you see that lot?"

He pointed to Bassanga's lot where we had had the big palaver about the parrot feathers. "We want to build that house after working hours as our gift to Bokotola. If you will have sand and cement put there, we will start immediately, just the two of us, and we will continue every afternoon until we have completely built the walls on that house."

"Of course I'm in agreement!" I said. "That's a beautiful idea. God bless both of you. That makes me happy beyond the words to express it!"

Mbomba and Pastor Lokoni meant what they said. They worked faithfully for over a month until they had completed their self-imposed task. Bassanga, the owner, came frequently to give them a hand. This contribution of labor was the equiva-

lent of a gift of over $100 to the Project. But much more than
the money, their contribution was a priceless gift to me personally, to the volunteers, and to the workmen and families of
Bokotola.

Before starting the first house at Bokotola, we had built a
small storage room and shed in the area designated as a park.
Under this shed we did a lot of our carpentry work. Within a
few weeks we had accumulated quite a supply of short pieces
of wood too short to make trusses, doors, or windows, but too
good to throw away.

Mbomba came to me with a suggestion: "Let's make furniture with that wood."

"That's a good idea," I responded. "Perhaps you can go into
partnership with the Project. You make items of furniture to
sell. We'll keep up with all the expenses, and divide the profits
50-50 between you and the Project. In that way, you can make
some money and the Project can make a profit, too."

He agreed happily, and Mbomba's furniture business was
born. He hired a carpenter, and within a matter of days they
were turning out beds, chairs, tables, and other household
items. He had a ready supply of customers among the families
moving into their new homes. Within two months he had to
add a second employee. Then a third. By the end of six
months, he had five employees.

I worked out a deal for him to make interior doors and
kitchen windows for the Project houses. As usual, Mbomba
wanted to go faster and faster. He did careful work and turned
out products more rapidly than other shops in town. Soon he
attracted the attention of the school authorities and began
getting contracts to make school desks. Later, he was even
being hired to put in windows and doors and to do other repair
work on the school buildings.

The shop soon outgrew the little shed in the park, so we
proposed a shop in his back yard. Chuck drew up a plan for a
building with two storage rooms and a big open-shed work
area. We built it, with Mbomba doing much of the work himself after hours. An agreement was drawn up to repay the cost
of the shop over a ten-year period: Mbomba would make the
payments each month along with his house payments.

Shortly before leaving Zaire, I turned the business over to
Mbomba as sole proprietor. The enterprise was solidly established, and he had fully demonstrated his ability to manage it.

Mbomba was a man who had needed a chance. When it
came, he had taken full advantage of it. Within less than three
years, he went from being a penniless *chomeur* (unemployed)
to being an employer with seven people on his payroll. From a

falling-down shack, he had moved into a decent house made of durable materials. From receiving no income, he had risen to a salary and income from his shop of over $200 a month—a very significant sum in Zaire. Under his direct supervision, a community of hundreds of people had sprung into existence right in the heart of Mbandaka. And through it all, he had retained his warm Christian character and the full portion of his humility and kindness.

Le Capita, Mbomba, *mon ami* (my friend). I shall always remember you as one of the finest men I've ever met.

11

Rise Up and Walk

"*DONNEZ-moi dix makutas*. (Give me ten makutas [10¢]."
Three men were in my yard. Each of them had only one leg.
One was leaning on his crutches at the far side of the front
yard. Another was sitting on the ground beside him. The third
man, also sitting on the ground, was in front of our door. As I
emerged from the house he looked up at me with pleading
eyes, his hand outstretched. He thrust it toward me each time
he softly and earnestly repeated, "*Donnez-moi dix makutas*."

We had been in Mbandaka less than a week. We were living
in another missionary's house until we could finish cleaning
and fumigating our own. It was Friday, the begging day. We
had already been told that the beggars would be around—
most of them one-legged fellows—every Friday.

Motioning to the other two men to come closer, I sat down
on the grass and began to talk with them. I questioned them
concerning how they had lost their legs, where they lived, how
they managed. I asked how many one-legged people there
were in the Mbandaka area. They didn't know for sure, but
thought there must be at least forty or fifty.

In our first few days in Mbandaka we had already been
confronted by desperate needs everywhere we turned; we felt
overwhelmed by the magnitude of the problems. Indeed, the
Block and Sand Project had more than enough problems to
keep us fully occupied. But we also knew that the only real
solution lay in helping the people to help themselves. Now, as I
talked to the men, I remembered a 1966 visit to the wooden leg
clinic at the ecumenical mission hospital at Kimpese, and I
wondered whether the terrible human need facing me might
not be one problem we *could* tackle. I asked the men if they
would like to have a wooden leg. Their reply was an enthusiastic and unanimous "Yes."

"However," I added, "if I help you get a wooden leg, there
will be no more handouts. You'll have to find a job. Do you
want to do that? Will you be willing to give up begging and go
to work if you get a new wooden leg?"

"Yes. Yes!"

"Fine. I'll see what I can do." I got up and turned to go back
into the house.

"Monsieur." I looked back over my shoulder. All of them again thrust upturned palms toward me. They were smiling and trying to look pitiful at the same time. I smiled back as I rammed my hand in my pocket and pulled out a few makutas for each man.

"Okay," I told them. "Here is something. Now I'll start working on getting you some new legs. Goodbye."

That same day I wrote to the Kimpese Hospital, *Institut Médical Evangélique*, asking prices and procedures for obtaining wooden legs. Their reply stated that the average cost for a leg, including all incidentals, would be approximately two hundred dollars. We could have casts of the stubs taken locally and send them, along with the required measurements, to the clinic at Kimpese. Wooden legs could be made from this information and shipped to us. Enclosed with the letter were printed forms to fill out for each person supplying his detailed dimensions: length of leg from crotch to knee, thigh circumference, length of the remaining foot, and so on.

I took all this material to Barbara Walker, a fellow missionary who had arrived in Zaire with her husband, Desmond, just two weeks ahead of us. Barbara was now directing the missionary clinic at nearby Bolenge. I explained the project and asked if she could take care of the casts and the measurements for each person. Her answer was Yes ... gladly.

Now we were all set to start the wooden-leg project except for one problem—we didn't have any money. So I began preparing the "begging letters."

In the meantime, more men were coming in as the word spread that we were a source for wooden legs. We compiled a list, noting the name, address, reason for loss of leg, and other pertinent information for each man. We told them that we could not start the program yet, but that they would be informed when we were ready to begin taking measurements.

Some of these amputations had been caused by accidents, but well over half of the people we worked with had lost their legs as a result of infection. In the tropics even the tiniest of sores can quickly become infected and develop into a serious problem. Time and again, people told us they had had a minor cut or a scratch which got worse and worse until the leg had to be cut off to save their life.

One of the first names to be put on our wooden-leg waiting list was that of Botschikala. He had been one of the three men in our front yard that first Friday. The next time he came to see us he asked me to help him get a pension from his former employer. He had been working for the company when he lost his leg two years earlier. At the time he had been promised some compensation, but had never been able to get anything. I copied addresses from the papers he had and promised to write to the capital about his situation. I gave him a date to return to the house for a reply.

A few days later he was back at our door. My initial reaction upon seeing him was a flash of irritation because he had come back too soon. He detected the tone of agitation in my voice, and tears welled up in his eyes. In broken French he began to tell me about another illness of some sort.

After a few minutes of struggling for words to explain his problem, he sensed that I was not fully comprehending and beckoned me to come with him behind a little wall next to the house. There he dropped his pants and began to unwind a dirty bandage from around the thigh above the stub of his leg. When he pulled off the last strip of cloth, I was rocked back on my heels by what I saw. Just below his crotch was a cruel, gaping hole, oozing pus and blood. The man's stub of a leg was about to rot off!

As I stood there viewing his pitiful condition, a sobering thought struck me. When I had been going through his papers a few days earlier, I had discovered that Botschikala was exactly my age. And I remembered what a professor had told our class of criminal law students years ago, as we drove up in a bus to the entrance of the Alabama State Prison.

"Men," he said, pointing to the high prison walls, "just remember as we visit these people that there but for the grace of God are you!"

I looked at this man and I saw *me*—but for the grace of God—slumped on the earth, penniless, one leg cut off and a terrible festering sore eating away at the stub, sitting on the edge of the grave.

I had an appointment with Pastor Boyaka for an hour later, but I told Linda to explain when the Pastor came that I had gone to seek medical attention for this man. Then we hurried to the Bolenge clinic to see Barbara Walker; as it was late in the afternoon we found her at her home.

When Botschikala revealed the sore to her, she gasped. It was as shocking to her as it had been to me. She almost cried as she told me there was practically nothing in the clinic with which to treat him. His condition, she said, was serious, but perhaps with proper treatment his life could be saved. We took him down to the clinic for a "halfway" treatment, and then I drove him home.

The following day I talked to Botschikala about going to the Kimpese hospital for treatment since there was not adequate medical care for a case like his in the Mbandaka area. I also told him that after his sore healed he could stay on at the hospital to have a new wooden leg made and fitted to his stub.

He agreed, but he wanted his wife to accompany him.

I bought boat tickets for them, and a couple of days later, when the next boat was scheduled to depart for Kinshasa, I drove them to the dock and gave them a letter to the hospital authorities and enough money for food along the way. In the letter I explained that I was a newly-arrived missionary in Mbandaka, and that I had gotten involved in an effort to secure wooden legs for the one-legged folk of the city. I told of signing this man up on our waiting list for a wooden leg, and then learning of his terrible sore.

I concluded: "I've undertaken to assist this man as a personal matter. Needless to say, I don't have unlimited resources to give you a blank check, but I don't want to see him die in the road for lack of proper medical attention. What is his condition? Is there hope for curing his leg? Do you have a policy for charity cases? Give me the facts about your procedures and his condition, and we'll see what we can work out. But please don't turn him out ..."

The hospital didn't have a charity program, but they didn't turn him out. They gave him the best treatment they had and allowed us to pay later.

In October of 1973 the hospital wrote: "Here is the latest news on Botschikala. The doctor treating him says he is reasonably sure that the sore on his stump is cancerous. He advises against a false leg for him ..."

In November I received a final letter informing us that they had discharged the patient because they were unable to do anything more for him. I heard nothing from Botschikala, and I can only assume he died soon thereafter.

Meanwhile, more and more men—and even a few women— were coming to sign up for wooden legs. To raise funds for this endeavor, I began mailing letters to friends at home. One such letter went to Doug McKee, pastor of the Edgerton United Methodist Church in Edgerton, Wisconsin:

... I believe in the scripture which says, "Ask, and you will receive." Today I am asking for a wooden leg for Ekofo Ilonga, age 37. He made his living as a fisherman until March of 1971, when he accidentally fell out of his boat, and before he could scramble back in, a big crocodile got his right leg just above the knee. He wants to be able to work again and support his family.

Like most people here, he has no money. There is a hospital at Kimpese, down near the ocean, that makes wooden legs, and the cost should be about two hundred dollars for everything. When Linda and I decided to start this wooden-leg project, the word began to get around, and now people come hobbling down the road to our house nearly every day, looking for their leg ...

In addition to Ekofo, some of the others who have come are: Bong-walanga Lokiyo, who got a small cut on his ankle which became infected and the leg had to be cut off. Lofenda Isalanza, who fell off a motorboat and had his leg severed by the propeller. Baende Ikolongano, a fourteen-year-old boy who lost his leg when a tractor-pulled lawn mower ran over him.

Some of these unfortunates have indicated that they can pay part of the cost. They just do not have enough money for everything. Will you and your people help with this undertaking? If you think you can, write me as soon as possible and I'll send you pictures and more complete details ...

The response was swift and encouraging. Doug McKee wrote: "I bring good tidings of great joy. ... The people of Edgerton know how to respond to needs. This week I will be sending a check, and I am sure there will be more ..."

There were many other generous responses. The United Church of Christ of Catasauqua, Pennsylvania, made a big wooden leg and the members literally stuffed it with money. Dave Coulter, campus minister at the University of Wyoming, organized "The Wooden Leg Theatre" and presented plays and dramatic readings for groups in many Wyoming towns and cities, raising hundreds of dollars for the project. My boyhood church in Lanett, Alabama, and my Aunt Irene's Methodist Church in Fairfax, Alabama, paid for a leg for the fourteen-year-old boy. Money for the very first leg was sent by our good friends Paul and Iris Horne of Houston, Texas. The Gemmer Christian Family Foundation contributed generously. Dick and Marylou Crooks of Sanbornton, New Hampshire, raised funds in their church and community for the project. Rufus King of Manchester College in Indiana contributed money for a leg. So did the Messiah Lutheran Church in Rockford, Illinois. Marge Hilty of Columbus Grove, Ohio, coordinated a successful fund-raising campaign in her Mennonite church. Dr. Bill Smith of Dayton, Ohio, headed an effort in his Presbyterian church for the one-legged folk. David and Bonnie Graber of Busby, Montana, shared in providing legs.

In the following months, the faithful contributions of these friends and many others made it possible for us to accept *every* person who came needing a new leg.

By early September of 1973 we were ready to take the first group of five men to the clinic to have casts made and measurements taken. They met at our house in Mbandaka one afternoon and we drove out to Bolenge about three o'clock. It was nearly six o'clock when all the procedures were completed. I gathered the five men, together with the little staff of the clinic, around me in the dusk. Speaking in French, with an interpreter for a couple of the men who did not understand that language, I explained that they were going to get new legs because there were Christians in Edgerton, Windermere, Evansville, Houston and other towns and villages in the United States who had heard of their need, and these Christians, because they had enough to share, wanted to help. I told the men I wanted them to share in this undertaking, too, because there were so many more who needed new legs.

When I said this, one of the men asked how much was expected of them. Before I could answer, Boyokola Emengala, who had had his leg shot off while in the Army twenty years earlier, responded.

"You give," he said, "according to your riches, as the others in America are giving." He had already given eight Zaires, and later he gave five more. In the months ahead some of the other men contributed to the Fund, but most did not. They simply did not have anything to give.

More people continued to come. By Christmas of 1973 twenty-six people had been signed up and measured for new legs. All of these measurements and casts were sent immediately to the Kimpese wooden-leg clinic ... but no legs were coming back. The men were getting impatient, and so were we. On January 4, 1974 I wrote the hospital:

When can we expect to start receiving some of the legs? Have you already shipped any? The people keep coming and asking when the legs are going to arrive. They are so anxious. Some have even gotten angry; they think maybe the whole project is a hoax of some sort ...

After months of waiting, a few legs began to arrive. Most of them did not fit properly. Also, many of the measurement forms were returned to us with the notation that for one reason or another the leg could not be made without more measurements. The complications seemed endless. When a leg had been severed below the knee, the patient frequently was unable to straighten it. He could not even be measured for a leg until therapy could help him straighten his stub.

A full year after the wooden-leg program had been initiated, over thirty people were signed up for new legs, but only seven had actually received them. We decided to give up making casts locally; we would simply send everybody to the clinic for measuring and fitting. Linda took over this program completely, sending two to four people every month to Kimpese— over five hundred miles by riverboat and train and bus—until everyone had been taken care of.

Engbondu Mosakui had been our first patient to require therapy before he could straighten his stub. We had provided money to send him to Kimpese with his wife to cook and care for him. One morning some weeks later I walked out our front door and there he was, beaming. The therapy had been a total success, and with his new leg he could walk nearly as smoothly as a normal person.

Engbondu had brought with him his little son, who was perhaps five years old. After talking happily for a few minutes, he pushed the boy toward me, saying that the child was mine to keep. He was so thrilled about his new leg that he wanted to give me his little boy!

I thanked him as profusely as I knew how, but declined his gift, saying I wasn't sure the little fellow would like that idea, and that I also thought it would be best for him to stay with his own family. The little boy shyly—and with evident relief— backed up against his father again, and Engbondu walked away proudly ... on two legs.

A few months later Ekofo Ilonga, the man whose leg had been bitten off by a crocodile, stopped by our house on his way home from Kimpese with his new leg. He stayed only a few minutes; he was in a hurry to return to his village to ask the witch doctor exactly why that crocodile had attacked him. Long afterward Ekofo came back to see us, and he recounted the witch doctor's explanation.

It seems that the spirits of his deceased mother and father had entered the crocodile, causing it to bite off his leg. His father, the witch doctor said, had been angry at Ekofo for not coming to see him when he was terminally ill. After the father died, he convinced his wife, who had died many years earlier, that she should cooperate with him to bite off one of their son's legs as punishment, and they had entered the crocodile and done their dirty work.

Ekofo was greatly alarmed by this story, for he didn't know what his dead parents' anger might cause them to do next. For a fee of five Zaires, the witch doctor agreed to stir up some medicine guaranteed to prevent the deceased parents from ever bothering him again. The money was paid and the matter was settled. Ekofo was satisfied. He had peace of mind.

I asked Ekofo if he was a Christian.

"Yes," he said, surprised that I would ask that question. "I am a Christian."

"You are a Christian and you believe your parents bit off your leg?"

"Yes, I believe that. No crocodile would have bitten off my leg if there had not been some reason. The witch doctor told me the true reason."

"When your parents were alive, did they love you?"

"Yes, they loved me."

"While they were alive, if they were angry with you would they have tried to cut one of your legs off?"

"No."

"Well, then, why do you think they would do this after they died?"

"I don't know, but they did. The witch doctor told me so."

"And you believe him?"

His face was full of puzzlement.

"Of course I believe him. He has healed many people in my village. He is a man who knows things like that."

I told him that I didn't believe his parents had caused the crocodile to bite his leg off, and that I thought the crocodile bit off his leg simply because that is the nature of crocodiles. He listened politely, but it was obvious that he found my simple explanation utterly ridiculous. Soon he walked off up the road, content both with his new leg and with his insurance against vindictive spirits.

As word spread about our project "Rise Up and Walk," people came from hundreds of miles away to sign up for a wooden leg. One of these was an attractive young woman named Andoni Montingea. Two years earlier she had been in the forest helping her husband cut trees. In the course of their work a tree had fallen on her, badly mangling her leg. They had had to paddle for two days in a dugout canoe to reach the hospital in Mbandaka. By that time infection had set in and it was too late to save the leg.

After the amputation, the husband had left her with their five small children—though he had caused her handicap, he didn't want a one-legged wife. An uncle in Mbandaka had allowed her to move in with him and there they managed to eke out a living.

The day she came to see us, we saw her at a distance, hopping toward the house. She had no walking stick or crutches. She just hopped a few steps, rested, and hopped a few steps more.

We described the plight of this unfortunate young mother to some friends we had met in Paris—the Monroes of Elmira, New York. Their teen-age daughter, Maggie, decided to accept the challenge of raising enough money for a new leg. Her youth group in the Elmira Baptist Church presented a play with all the proceeds designated for Andoni, and the new leg was paid for.

In October of 1974, Linda sent Andoni to Kimpese with a letter of introduction. Andoni was fitted with a leg, and before Christmas she was back in Mbandaka wearing the new leg and walking normally. It gave her a new lease on life. She could easily manage to take care of her children, work in the garden ... and go to church. She had not been a Christian before, but soon after returning to Mbandaka she was baptized and became very active in the life of her church.

Each person's leg problem was an individual one, and Linda ran into all sorts of hassles trying to get the people down to Kimpese. Here is Linda's account:

After all the arrangements had been made with the patient, his family, and the clinic, there were bound to be further complications—for example, in buying the boat tickets. The officials at the port never knew for sure when the riverboat would be coming in.

"It should be here Wednesday or Thursday," they would say, but they refused to sell any tickets until they had a radio message from the captain giving his exact time of arrival. Frequently I would have to go to the port as many as ten or twelve times just to find out when the boat would arrive.

When definite word was finally received, tickets were put on sale immediately. Hordes of people crowded around the one little barred window, with everyone pushing and shoving. Once I saw a man's shirt ripped off his back while he was at the window buying his ticket as others were scuffling to be next.

Sometimes word would filter into the ticket office that a *mundele* lady was waiting and they would allow me to enter the office and buy a ticket from the man seated behind a desk. I would hand him the slip of paper with the person's name on it and request a ticket to Kinshasa. Usually at that point he would be distracted by someone else ... and someone else ... and someone else. When my patience was at its outer limits, he would hand me the ticket and I would be off to get our one-legged friend and help him or her onto the boat.

Getting one-legged Mondo Bolenga on the riverboat was a real ordeal ... with a touching ending. On the day before she was scheduled to leave for Kinshasa, she hobbled down the road to our house with the aid of a crude walking stick. She had come from her home at the leper colony about fifteen miles south of Mbandaka. We fed her supper and prepared a bed for her in our living room.

The next morning a man arrived to help her carry her small bundle of belongings to the riverboat. The three of us piled into our little Volkswagen and drove to the port, where I left them to wait. I gave the ticket to the man to hold for her, promising to come back in an hour to see if the boat had arrived.

When I returned, the boat had already docked and people were streaming aboard. Mondo was standing alone.

"Where's your friend?" I inquired urgently. "Where's your ticket?"

"He's got my ticket," she replied. "He went off looking for food and hasn't come back."

I just about panicked. What could I do—buy another ticket? No! I was sure they had all been sold. I'd better go looking for the man.

I jumped into the car and raced up and down the nearby streets, peering into all the little stores and markets. I couldn't find him. I drove back to the port. Mondo was no longer standing where I had left her. Thinking she might have gone down to the boat to try to get on board, I rushed through the gates, hurriedly explaining the situation to the reluctant guards.

Just at that moment there was a break in the crowd, and I saw Mondo. She was crawling up the gangplank on her hands and knees, fighting through the confusion of pushing passengers and bleating goats. Her friend was standing at the foot of the gangplank. While I had been hunting him, he had returned with the ticket and the food.

As Mondo finally scrambled into the crowded boat, tears came to my eyes to see that pathetic sight, and to realize how much she was willing to go through to get to Kimpese for that new leg.

In addition to sending people to the Kimpese clinic as they arrived, Linda was also responsible for paying our bills there. Periodically, the hospital accounting office would send us a bill and we would transfer that amount to its Kinshasa bank account. Always before, when these bills arrived, there had been enough money to pay them.

But one day in June of 1975 Linda gravely asked me, "Millard, do you know how much we owe the hospital in Kimpese?"

"No. How much?"

"Twenty-seven hundred dollars!"

Those travel expenses, therapy, operations, food, and wooden legs had mounted up to more than we had realized. I got out the typewriter—it was time to beg again!

As before, the response was swift and generous. Good friends Elmer and Anna Lushbough of Baker, Montana, organized a unique slipper knitting project. Anna wrote: "With orders for eight more pairs of slippers, here is enough to buy a second limb, Linda. Orders are slackening—our town is getting 'slippered up,' as our grandchildren say. We're just glad the people here could use that many! Elmer still knits as he listens to the evening news ... "

Loren Ceder, a prosthetist in Tacoma, Washington, sent a large and unexpected check, prompted by the article I had written in *Faith at Work* Magazine. Gifts from other friends kept arriving; we soon got out of debt and were able to continue accepting all the candidates who came for wooden legs.

As each person returned from Kimpese with a new wooden leg, he was given a Bible in a brief presentation service at our house or at his, or during Sunday worship at the church in his neighborhood. We always explained that the leg was made possible through the generosity of God's people. If you are thankful for your new leg, we added, return thanks and praises to God. And if you are able to do so, you are encouraged to contribute to the Fund so that even more people can receive new legs.

One of these men, Bofanga Bosange, was given his Bible in a simple ceremony in our front yard. Then, a year later, he was given a second Bible at Bokotola when the families there received Bibles as part of the inauguration ceremonies for the new community. He had been chosen for a Bokotola house only a few months after he got his new leg. With a new leg and a new house, Bofanga was really sitting on top of the world. He acquired a bicycle and I often saw him pedaling about town. Whenever he spotted me he would throw up a hand and wave vigorously, grinning from ear to ear.

Bofanga was one happy fellow, as was I. Seeing the tangible, exciting results of our wooden-leg project was one of the great rewards of service in Zaire.

12

In the Prison

DREDGING sand—making blocks—repairing machinery—building houses—distributing eyeglasses and wooden legs. Six days a week I was deeply involved in many areas of service, but I had planned to take Sundays off for worship, rest, and fellowship with my family.

Pastor Lokoni, however, had other ideas. Not long after we had arrived in Zaire, he invited me to spend a Sunday afternoon with him. What he had in mind was not exactly a relaxed outing. Instead, it was a visit to the Mbandaka Central Prison, where he served as pastor. From that time on, we went together to the prison every Sunday, and those worship services became an important part of my week.

The prison itself was a big, ugly box with walls of loud, glossy blue. The roof had been painted many years earlier, but one could no longer tell what color it had been. Inside, there was a large courtyard with rooms opening onto it from four sides. In the center of the courtyard two long open-sided sheds shaded prisoners from the blazing tropical sun.

The atmosphere inside the building was grim. Years before, the walls had been painted white, but now they were covered with smears of dirt and smoke. The rooms where the men slept at night were totally black. There were no beds, no tables, no chairs ... nothing. Just grime and dreariness.

Most of the men were scantily clad in rags. They sat around staring blankly into space or chatting in small groups. Some paced up and down the courtyard, while others tended little fires over which they were preparing some morsel of food.

At the far end of the courtyard from the main entrance gate was a larger room, with a wide opening leading into it. Inside, the walls were scarred from years of being scratched by hundreds of men with nothing else to do. On one side someone had painted a nearly life-sized cowboy complete with ten-gallon hat and holstered pistol. On the back wall was the faint outline of a cross, but the paint was so old and faded that one had to look hard for it in order to see it. The floor had once been concrete, but only a few patches of crumbling cement were left, with the remainder of the floor being plain dirt. The ceiling had turned jet black from years of accumulated smoke.

Everything in the room was grimy. This was the prison "church."

When we arrived on Sunday afternoon for the service, we were ushered through the main entrance by one of the soldiers on duty. Then we made the long walk through the center of the courtyard to the church. As we walked along, Pastor Lokoni repeated over and over in a loud voice, "Come to the church service. Everybody come to the church service!" People began to fall in beside and behind us, each one extending his hand and greeting us cheerfully. By the time we arrived at the church, we would already have a fairly large congregation following us.

Within a few minutes, someone would come through the main entrance gate with a table and two or three chairs. These were brought into the church and set up front as a "pulpit" and chairs for the visitors. We frequently brought singing groups, guest speakers, and other visitors; Ken Sauder, in particular, took a big part in the prison ministry. All of us were given chairs—everyone else stood along the walls or sat on the floor. Women prisoners, who were brought over from an adjoining building, sat in a group near the front of the room.

In the courtyard, just in front of the entrance, there was usually a man standing at rigid attention. He wore only a flimsy cloth around his loins, and on his head was a metal pot. He kept his eyes glued on the principal activity of the moment, but he never changed his expression, and he never participated in any other way in the service. He was one of the many mental cases in the prison. There were even children no more than twelve years old along with the grown men and the mentally deranged.

Pastor Lokoni always started the service with a Scripture reading followed by lively congregational singing. And did the people ever sing! They seemed to be releasing long-pent-up feelings as they belted out the familiar Christian hymns.

When we brought special singing groups the attendance doubled, and if the people really liked a particular song they clapped and cheered. From time to time the prisoners themselves formed musical groups and performed during the service.

Pastor Lokoni and I shared the preaching responsibilities. When I spoke, he translated my French into Lingala since not all of the prisoners understood French. Following the benediction we always stood in the courtyard in front of the church, and people crowded around to ask about Bibles, eyeglasses, stamps, medicine, and other things. We represented one of their few contacts with the outside, and they tried to hold onto us and press us into service for whatever need they might have.

One Sunday soon after I joined Pastor Lokoni—it was the last Sunday before Christmas—I saw a young man struggling toward me through the crowd. As he came closer I recognized him as Dongo, one of the new workers in the Block and Sand Project. I had hired him about six weeks earlier to unload sand from the barges onto the dump truck. I hadn't seen him for two weeks, however, as the boat that pushed the barges in from the crane in the river had broken down, and as a result that crew hadn't been working.

His appearance shocked me. He was thinner than when I had last seen him. His whole countenance was downcast and dejected.

"What are you doing here?" I asked.

"I couldn't pay my taxes because I haven't been able to find work since the boat broke down, and they came and put me in prison three days ago," he replied.

"How much tax do you owe?"

"Four Zaires."

"And they put you in prison for *that*?"

"Yes."

"For how long?"

"Two months."

My pocket burned and my hand itched to pull out the four Zaires and free this man. But dozens of others were crowding around and asking for money. So I simply looked long and hard into his forlorn eyes. Then I shook his hand and said, "*Au revoir.*"

"*Au revoir. Merci. Merci.*" and he bowed to me.

"Thank you!" Thank you for what, I wondered. I hadn't given him a cent. I hadn't even given him a promise. But I suppose he could see in my eyes that I cared about his plight. He was thanking me for that. That tiny gesture of kindness was an important thing to him.

I buzzed away from the prison on my motorbike with Pastor Lokoni mounted behind me. I rode in total silence, absorbed in my thoughts about this young worker. I hadn't developed a personal relationship with him, but I *had* come to appreciate his warm spirit and his diligent work. Of the ten new men, he was probably the most conscientious.

I pondered his fragile financial situation, which was so typical in Mbandaka. Four Zaires from prison—or one could just as easily say four Zaires from starvation. This episode made a tremendous impact on me, because I had been so full of happiness for the past two days since Chris and Kim had arrived home for the Christmas holidays. We had a party planned for that afternoon right after the prison service. But there, in stark contrast to my joy, was this young man in prison for the lack of four Zaires! He was hungry—the prisoners never got enough to eat—and scared, and lonely.

I just couldn't ride away and leave him there. His situation was too close to me, too urgent. I stopped the motorbike and turned to Pastor Lokoni.

"Pastor, we've got to get Dongo out of prison. Would you be willing to go back and pay his fine if I gave you the four Zaires? I believe you could handle the matter better than I could."

"Yes, I'll be glad to do it."

Thus we liberated this young man, but I couldn't bail them all out. In this one prison, Dongo told me, there were at least ten others who were serving time for want of a few Zaires to pay their taxes. And there were so many others, in prison and out, who were suffering in countless ways for lack of a pitifully small sum of money!

As I continued on my way home for the Christmas party, I couldn't shake this off. I kept thinking over and over—those of us who call ourselves Christians cannot be worthy of that name unless we continuously wrestle with the gross injustices which put the Dongos of this world behind bars or in a grave for lack of a few Zaires.

At the party later that afternoon I tried to convey my deep feeling about what had happened, but I couldn't talk much because of my tears.

A few months later, I learned the dismal situation at the Central Prison had put a man in his grave. On that Sunday morning Faith, our seven-year-old daughter, had gone to the prison with us. She wanted to visit a Belgian woman who was charged with killing her husband. Faith had never met the woman, but she knew the children, who attended the same school she did. Faith felt sorry for the woman, locked up in the prison, and wanted to take her a box of cookies.

When we arrived at the prison, Pastor Lokoni was informed that a prisoner had died earlier that morning, and his family wanted us to pray with them. The man's body had been taken outside the prison to the nearby house of a brother, so Pastor Lokoni and I left to visit with this family, while Faith went into the prison with a soldier to see the Belgian woman.

Accompanied by half a dozen men, Pastor Lokoni and I walked down a narrow dusty road and across a little field of rice and corn to the one-room shack of the brother of the deceased. It was a heartbreaking scene that met us when we entered.

The palm branch roof of the house was collapsing, and the floor still had mud puddles from the last rain. The dead man was lying on a rickety straw bed in the middle of the room. A few leaves were stuck in the two corners of the bed nearest his head, and his body was covered with a dingy blanket. Only his feet and head were exposed. A large green fly was busily exploring his nose, crawling first up one nostril and then the other. Around the walls and in the single doorway leading into the house, men, women and children sat hunkered down, quiet and somber.

We stood silent for a few moments, and then the Pastor began to pray. The dead man's brother, standing at his elbow, began to cry, at first softly and then in heaving sobs. After the prayer, Pastor Lokoni went slowly around the room saying a few gentle words of comfort to each person. Then we stooped down to go out the door and return to the prison.

Just at that moment Faith ran up to us.

"Daddy, where is the dead man? I want to see him."

I took her by the hand and led her back into the house, and she stood at the foot of the makeshift bed, silently studying the smooth lifeless face.

After a moment she turned to me and asked, "Daddy, why did he die?"

"Diarrhea," I said.

"Diarrhea? But, Daddy, people don't die with diarrhea!"

"That's right, Faith. They don't if they have proper treatment, but if they're poor and can't get medicine, they frequently die."

She didn't reply. We walked in silence back into the prison for the service. Nothing else was said about the experience until that night when I was tucking her in bed.

"Daddy," she said, gazing into my eyes, "I'm sorry these people are so poor out here."

I will always remember her sadness, so simple and yet profound. It was the pure sadness of a little child. She could see clearly that something is badly wrong in a world where a relatively young man dies a senseless death from something that could easily be cured by available, inexpensive medicines.

In spite of the depressing atmosphere of the prison, there were many moments of joy. One of the most heartwarming occurred just two weeks after the episode with Dongo. The service that Sunday was really special, with two visiting singers and Don Mosley (who had just arrived to do the surveying for Bokotola) participating. Don preached in English, which I translated into French, and Pastor Lokoni finished in Lingala.

After the service, as we were walking through the courtyard toward the main gate, one of the women prisoners came up between Don and me and gently took my hand; then, after a few seconds, she took Don's hand also. She walked with us, hand in hand, right up to the gate. There, with an absolutely glowing, radiant smile, she gripped our hands tightly in hers, pulled them together up in front of her face, and kissed them. It was, I think, the most beautiful "thank you" I've ever experienced—a truly unforgettable moment. My heart was aglow for days thereafter from that simple act of love and affirmation.

Preaching to the prisoners came to be a joy to me. At first it was a real chore trying to think of something to say to people in such a pitiful situation. I had spoken to literally hundreds of gatherings throughout the United States and Canada, but never had I been called upon to address a group like this— poverty-stricken, and imprisoned as well. But, as I searched the New Testament, I found a wealth of hope and encouragement for people in just their situation.

One such treasure, which meant much to the prisoners, was the story of the Gadarene demoniac (Luke 8: 26–39). I used this story to point out God's great love for a little insignificant—by the world's standards—crazy boy, and His willingness to sacrifice two thousand hogs—a considerable economic investment—for the boy's salvation. In the twinkling of an eye the boy was transformed from a wild-eyed maniac who would not wear clothes, and who had lost all meaningful contact with humanity, into a person in his right mind.

What brought about his great and sudden change? I asked. Simply *Jesus*. Face-to-face confrontation with Him inevitably means radical change. He is always waiting for us to come, as the demoniac ran to Him, and all are acceptable to Him, regardless of their station in life.

I noted that the world's mentality is directly opposed to that of Jesus, and that this difference is illustrated by the hog owners, who were devastated by the loss of their hogs but were not the least bit concerned with the boy's salvation. Indeed, their reaction to this tremendous event was to demand that Jesus leave their territory immediately.

I concluded the meditation by calling on the prisoners to turn their minds and hearts to the living Christ and ask Him to fill them with His spirit and love. In so doing, I said, they would be set free through the change within them, and the most that the prison authorities—or anyone else, for that matter—could do from that point on would be to lock up their bodies. Their minds and spirits would have been liberated through salvation in Christ.

One Sunday in the prison I encountered a young man who reminded me very much of the Gadarene demoniac. When we walked through the main gate that day, a youth of about twenty was being held by two other prisoners. He was bellig-

erent and nearly uncontrollable, and behaved as if he wanted
to attack us. The two men holding him began to drag him away
as he kicked and struggled. When they reached a door they
wanted him to go through, he suddenly became totally submis-
sive and lay on the ground sobbing. We walked past him to the
church room for the worship service.

After the songs and prayers, I stood up to speak. At this
point, the young man came crawling into the room on his
elbows and knees. He assumed a fetal position near the wall
and lay there sniffling and sobbing throughout my talk. He
appeared to be strong and healthy in every way except for his
tormented mind, and I fervently wished I could touch him
somehow with the healing power of God.

Another wish I felt constantly in the prison was for more
Bibles. At the very first service, the men began to plead for
Bibles. There were nearly five hundred prisoners in the prison
... and only one ragged, beat-up Bible.

During the week following that first service, I went to the
defunct church bookstore and found a small supply of Lingala
Bibles in the storage room. I got ten of them, and the following
Sunday we took them to the prison to distribute to the most
faithful participants in the worship service.

The prisoners who got the Bibles were jubilant, but a loud
clamor arose from the others. The next week I went back to
the bookstore and got fifty more Bibles. The next Sunday, as
we tried to give these out, however, the men became quite
boisterous, and the situation nearly got out of hand. Some men
who did not receive a Bible pleaded with us to the point of
tears.

The following week we brought ten more Bibles. The men
began to fight each other to get one, snatching and grabbing in
a wild melee. The prison authorities rushed in and confiscated
them. No longer would we be allowed to distribute Bibles—it
was too dangerous. So we left the last batch with the authorities to be put in the small prison library. There were no
more Bibles in the church bookstore or anywhere else in
Mbandaka, and the authorities told us that only if we had one
for every prisoner could we give them out again.

About this time Dr. Robert Nelson, Africa Secretary for the
Disciples, came to Mbandaka on his annual visit. I told him of
our need. I also told him I would like to have Bibles for the
families at Bokotola; I had already reserved a small supply
from the bookstore for the one-legged folk.

He replied without hesitation: "Bible money we've got! The
Division will be happy to provide the funds."

A few weeks later we placed the order. Three months went by ... six months ... a year ... still no Bibles.

In May of 1975, the Zaire Government suddenly banned religious services in the prison. We arrived as usual one Sunday afternoon and the authorities turned us back. They had received a telegram from the capital: religious services for prisoners were henceforth prohibited. That decision really saddened us; we knew those gatherings were the highlight of their monotonous week. And only two weeks earlier we had given the prisoners paint for their "church." They had made it fresh and attractive—and now they couldn't use it. The Bibles for the prisoners still had not arrived. Now we wondered how we could distribute them even if they did.

The same week the prison services were suspended, we did receive about a thousand Bibles in the Lonkundo tongue for general distribution in the city. The Bibles were given free, but we had to charge five cents each to cover shipping costs.

The first day of distribution, I took a supply to Pastor Lokoni to sell at Bokotola. As we were unloading the boxes from the truck a mechanic I knew walked by and saw them. He ran over and asked eagerly if he could buy one.

"Yes," I replied, "the price is five makutas."

He pulled out the money and excitedly poked it into Pastor Lokoni's hand. When he got his Bible he turned on his heel, took about three steps, and suddenly fell to his knees in prayer. It was such a dramatic thing I turned speechless to Ikete who was standing with us.

He smiled and explained, "He's wanted a Bible for a long time and couldn't get one. Now he is thanking God for his good fortune this morning."

Within less than a week all the Bibles had been sold, but for weeks thereafter people continued to plead for them. There is a great hunger in Zaire for God's word—someone could have a fantastic ministry in that part of Africa simply distributing Christian literature.

In January of 1976, fifteen months after they were ordered, the Bibles for the prisoners arrived. We contacted prison authorities. No, they replied, you may not enter the prison for this purpose, but you may leave the Bibles with us and we will distribute them. The prison director and his subordinates were apologetic about the rule banning services in the prison, but they had to follow the directives from Kinshasa.

One of the assistant directors had received a new house at Bokotola. We knew him well and had confidence in him to distribute the Bibles honestly. So Pastor Lokoni, Joe Kirk and I drove out one afternoon and unloaded the cartons on the ground in front of the director's office, specifically requesting that our friend be given the job of distributing them to the prisoners. We left Bibles for the guards as well, plus a few extras for the prison library, since we had been told that the ones we had left the year before had disappeared.

A few days later we saw the assistant director who gave out the Bibles, and he reported that the people were thrilled beyond words. They were praying for the day when we could come back to hold services. Those prison doors remained closed, however, for the duration of our stay in the country.

My memories of the prison ministry will always be filled with an indescribable combination of depression, thanksgiving, and joy. Our prayer continues to be that in the future those firmly bolted doors will once again be opened for the sharing of God's love.

13
"My House"

THE Lingala word for "house" is *ndako*. *Na* is the word for "of"; *ngai* means "me" or "my." Together, *ndako na ngai* is "house of me," or "my house." While we were building Bokotola, I heard that expression literally thousands of times. "I need my house," people said, pleading for one at Bokotola. "I do not have my house for my family." The fortunate ones who were selected for a new house would repeatedly point to their lot: "There is the place of my house!" After construction was started, they would return again and again, exclaiming, "It will be my house!" When the building was finally completed, the exclamation came louder than ever: *"Ndako na ngai!* (That's my house!)"

On several occasions I watched people standing out front, gazing at their new homes. One man especially was frequently in the street, just looking. He was Ilanga, a big, jolly nurse at the Mbandaka hospital. He and his family were living in a mud shack when I first met him, and when he applied for a new house at Bokotola he was chosen to receive the second one. Every time I saw him after that, he would break into joyous laughter and exclaim over and over, *"Merci, merci!* I am soon going to have a decent house to live in. *Merci, merci!"*

When the house was finished, he christened it *La Plus Belle Maison* ("The Most Beautiful House"). Everywhere he went he told people he lived in "The Most Beautiful House." "I find it most difficult to believe," he would say. "I shake my head, close my eyes, and open them again to see if the house is still there. I never thought I would live in a house like that."

Another man who was often in the street staring at his new home was Eseba. He was a mechanic. Nearly every time I saw him he would say, "Mr. Fuller, God exists. There is no other explanation for this house. I praise and thank Him for what has happened to me and my family."

These houses, which were the objects of so much praise and thanksgiving, were the ultimate in simplicity. But they were solidly built, and would not need to be rebuilt and repaired every few months as did the flimsy native huts. Living in a house of concrete block walls and a tin roof, people could be free of this burden, and their energy could be directed to other things.

One week end I had a personal experience of what life can be like in a mud shack. I went into the interior on a hunting trip and stayed in the home of one of the village families. During the night a driving storm hit the area. The wind, rain, and thunder woke me up, and I lay in bed wondering if the fragile house would stand the beating it was receiving.

Suddenly there was a rumble behind me. I grabbed the flashlight and shone it on the wall at the head of the bed just in time to see that side of the room come crashing to the ground. I ran to the far corner and spent the rest of the night, shivering, trying to avoid the driving pellets of rain that now poured down in unabated fury. Daylight was a long time in coming.

In Mbandaka after every rainstorm we heard tales of houses which had fallen down. Living in those tropical huts is not so romantic as people may think.

Mud houses are also havens and breeding places for all sorts of vermin and parasites. When Larry Stoner and I took the long trip to Lokole to visit the church coffee plantation, we slept with villagers along the way. One night, as we were settling into our cots, there was a flurry of excitement in the roof above us. Bits of straw and other debris came tumbling down. When we turned our flashlight toward the commotion, we saw a whole raft of bats scrambling after one another in the palm branches, causing the stuff to fall down on us. I got up and whacked at the creatures, but it was impossible to chase them out without destroying the roof. I wanted to move the bed to a new location, but the room was too small. So I crawled back onto the cot, pulled the sheet up over my head, and concentrated hard on being tired and sleepy. That was another long night.

What kind of health can people expect to have when living under these conditions? Lice fall out of the roof; worms infect the damp earthen floor; while other disease-carrying insects and microbes are imbedded overhead, underfoot, and in all four walls. And everywhere mosquitoes, swarming in through the cracks, suck your blood all night long, at the same time infecting you with malaria.

No! A picturesque native mud hut is not as romantic as it looks on a colored post card. The people who live in them know, and they desperately want to get out, into a house made of solid, lasting materials.

We started the Bokotola houses with a sturdy foundation trench dug to the depth necessary to find hard, solid soil. We dug the foundation trench for the outside walls with a width of 60 centimeters, and it was usually poured to a depth of 20 centimeters. We used cement, sand, and small red stones called *"limonete"* (these were readily available in Equator Region) for the foundations. We used no construction steel except in places where the soil was particularly boggy. In those cases we threw in rods of steel to strengthen the foundation at specific points.

Outside walls were built of concrete blocks 15 centimeters wide; for inside walls we used blocks of 10 centimeters. We "struck" the joints on all these blocks—that is, we cleaned the joints between the blocks as we laid them, and, using a small, slightly curved piece of metal, made a slight indentation in the cement. This gave an attractive appearance to the walls. Also, when the house was finished, the blocks were painted both inside and outside.

To us, the practice was not a new one—many houses in the United States are finished thus—but in Mbandaka such a thing was unheard of. Everyone just "slopped" the blocks into place and later plastered the walls, inside and out, with a cement mixture called *"crepesage."* This procedure was time-consuming and costly. By simply striking the joints and leaving the walls to be painted, we saved several hundred dollars and many man-hours of work on each house.

By the time we had completed a couple of houses, people were coming from all over the city, and even farther, to see this revolutionary way of finishing walls. Several months later the Government itself built a series of new schools in the area, and all of them were built with our struck joints!

Another technique we introduced was our method of building lintels over the doors and windows. The local practice was to pour these lintels in place. In other words, the blocks were built up to the height of the top of the doors and windows; then forms were built over the openings; steel rods were placed in these forms; then concrete was poured in. A couple of days later, the forms were ripped away, leaving the lintels in place for continuing the block work. In many instances a form would be built for the entire outer walls, holding steel rods and concrete. The idea behind this practice was to have a sturdy belt of steel and concrete around the structure. Such a procedure was useful for a multistoried house, but for single-story structures it was a waste of time and money.

We replaced these local methods with the simple practice of making two forms on the ground—one form was 10 centimeters wide for the lintels on the interior walls, and one was 15 centimeters wide for lintels on the exterior walls. We could control the quality of the lintels; we could pour them much faster; and we could use the forms over and over again. As they had with the struck joints, people came from far and wide to see this new way of pouring and placing lintels.

The local way of pouring floors is one thing we did not change. At Koinonia we had always done the floor before we built the walls, but here the practice was to pour the floor after the walls were up and the roof on. I asked several local builders about this and they all said this procedure was followed because of the hot sun. If the floor had been poured out in the open and left exposed to the sun, it would begin to crack.

After the galvanized tin roof was on, we poured each floor in a blitz job. Sand was piled just outside the house one afternoon. The following morning, the masons and their boy helpers arrived very early and started pouring the floor. This job was paid for by the task, not the hours, and the men were free to leave as soon as they finished. Everybody worked at fever pitch, because going home early was a highly desired thing. Usually by noon the floor was completely finished.

Local workmen also had their own method of mixing cement. The product was left very dry, with barely enough water to hold the sand and cement together. This was carted into the house in wheelbarrows and dumped on the ground, where it was leveled and packed down. The masons then poured small quantities of water on this packed cement mixture, producing a smooth, glossy surface with their trowels.

Ceilings went up next. We used an asbestos material which, like our other supplies, was often difficult to get, but which helped significantly in insulating the rooms from the blazing tropical sun.

Next came the doors and windows. These were all made locally by Mbomba or by Boango, the church builder, who had his own carpentry business, or in the church's woodworking shop in town. Glass was often nearly impossible to find for the windows, and wood was substituted in several of the houses. Solid wooden windows were always installed in the kitchens. These could be opened for ventilation during the day and securely locked against thieves at night.

Finally we did the painting. Families were requested to scrape off all the excess cement from the interior and exterior walls and to cover them with lime, which we furnished. Then our own workers, including Fuller children on school vacations, painted the houses inside and out.

The families themselves helped with their houses in many ways. Initially, they were requested to clear their lot of grass, weeds, bushes, and roots. After the walls were up, families were asked to put in the fill dirt and broken blocks to prepare for the floor. Finally it was their responsibility to dig the hole for their toilet. We always laid off the toilets in a straight line on the backs of the lots, but the families did the actual digging.

The project installed no pipes for plumbing or wiring for electricity. However, several families put in electrical wiring themselves in hopes that one day electricity would be brought into Bokotola by the city. One year after we started building, the city water and electricity department came in and installed water mains in all the streets of the area—but later they abandoned the project without ever connecting the houses into the system.

In the beginning, we built three-, four-, five-, and six-bedroom houses. Each house also had a living room, dining room, hallway, and kitchen. The houses were 7.8 meters wide and varied in length from 9.50 meters to 14 meters. The bedrooms were 3 meters square, with one bedroom being 4 meters by 3 meters. Within a year, however, runaway inflation forced us to make changes. Cement increased in price from $1.60 a sack to $2.90. Construction wood increased from $55 a cubic meter to $130. Tin went from $4.00 a sheet to $6.00. Roofing nails increased from $50 a case to $180!

We were forced to quit building the five- and six-bedroom houses, and I asked Chuck Clark to work on modifications which would save money without rendering the houses too small for the families. Chuck's careful designs produced suitable three- and four-bedroom houses which were only six meters wide. The hall was eliminated. The original models of three- and four-bedroom houses were reduced in width to 7.5 meters and in length about half a meter. The windows, which had been six blocks high, were now five. We reduced the width of the roof overhang from one meter to 70 centimeters and eliminated the ceiling material we had been putting under this overhang. The width of the facia (trim) boards decreased from 20 centimeters to 15.

These changes were absolutely necessary, because while building materials had more than doubled in price, salaries had increased only about 5 per cent. Families simply could not afford to pay twice the former monthly payments.

One room we did not change was the kitchen. From the beginning, the kitchens were separate from the main part of the house. Sometimes the separation was complete, with a covered walkway between the main house and the kitchen. At other times the kitchen was physically connected to the main part of the house, but it always had an outside door. In order to go into the kitchen it was necessary to walk out of the house and then, from the outside, to enter the kitchen.

This feature was extremely important to the Zairois style of meal preparation. With rare exceptions, the women cook over an open fire either on the ground or on the floor. If the kitchen is inside, within a few weeks the entire house will be black with smoke. But with the kitchen separate, that one room is soon blackened, of course, but the rest of the house remains clean. We also installed ventilation blocks around the top of the kitchen walls, thus allowing smoke to escape.

The women were literally thrilled with their kitchens—because we built them to conform to their way of doing things. The kitchens had none of the essentials of an American kitchen; there were no counters, cabinets, or drawers. There were only four walls and a floor, with a little storage room in the back, but that simple arrangement was precisely what they wanted.

Many Bokotola families moved into this kitchen as soon as it was finished, and did their cooking outside. They were so anxious to get out of their shacks that they didn't want to wait. Living in the unfinished house, they could also help even more with the final construction work.

Some families, strangely enough, did not move in even when their house was completely finished. This happened with the fifth house. When it was finished and the family did not enter, I went to the man and asked why.

"Oh," he replied, "you haven't finished some work."

"What work?" I asked.

He named three or four small items. I told him to meet me at his house later that day, and we would see exactly what had not been completed. This he did, pointing out a couple of joints that had not been properly filled with cement and a window that needed a bit more paint. We immediately took care of his complaints.

Days went by, and he still did not move in. Finally, I went to see him again.

"Why aren't you moving in now?" I asked.

"I don't have any curtains and I don't want to move in without curtains."

"Why not use the curtains that you have in the house where you live?"

"I don't have any curtains there."

"Well, why do you feel you must have curtains in the new house before you move in?"

"I wouldn't want to live in a nice house like that without curtains. Anyway, people could look in and see me. I couldn't stand that."

A few weeks later I was in Pastor Boyaka's office. He asked why this man had not moved in. I explained that his latest reason was that he had no curtains. Pastor Boyaka exploded.

"No curtains! I loaned him money weeks ago for the express purpose of buying curtains. I must talk to him about that. Having that house sit there empty is an embarrassment to the church with so many hundreds of people pleading for houses. He should move in."

More days went by, and still the man didn't move in. One day I saw him in the road in front of his house. I walked over to him, but before I could speak he blurted out, "Mr. Fuller, my house is badly situated."

"Your house is badly situated? What do you mean?"

"It is located between my two enemies!"

I couldn't believe my ears. "Your enemies? Why, the man on one side of you is the one who suggested your name to have a house. The other man is the one who built your house!"

"Yes, but they have changed. They are slandering my name because I don't move in."

We talked on and on, but I soon saw there was no budging him. Finally I walked away.

In the weeks to come, he tried to get various other people to swap houses with him, but no one would do so. I discussed the situation with Pastor Boyaka, and he promised to talk with the man again, but I don't think that he ever did. I decided to forget the whole thing. The man was making his monthly payments, and we had no basis on which to take the house from him.

Finally, six months later, he moved in—without curtains! In the weeks to come he made peace with his neighbors—who had never considered themselves his enemies, anyway. We never knew what changed his mind.

Soon after this house was finished, we completed the seventh one, and that family didn't move in, either. I began to inquire about them. No one knew of any reason why they shouldn't enter. Then one day the man came to the project with white spots of paint all over his face.

"What's that for?" I asked.

"My wife just had twins. It is our custom to paint our face like this when we have twins in the family."

"Well, congratulations! But why not move into your new house with those new babies?"

"I'll move in right after the twentieth of the month. That's when I get paid, and I will need the money for moving all my things."

But the twentieth came and went and he didn't appear. A month went by. One day Pastor Boyaka came over to the project and I asked him to speak to this man about moving in. (I had two pressing reasons for wanting people to move in as soon as a house was finished: First of all, it seemed almost obscene to have a nice house sitting empty for weeks and months when we were totally surrounded by hundreds of families living in miserable shacks. Secondly, I was afraid vandals would break into the house and wreck it.)

"He's over there at the house right now." Boyaka replied. "I saw him when I drove up. I'll walk over and talk to him about it."

A few minutes later, he came walking back with a big smile on his face. "He's not moving in because of those twins. He didn't want to tell you that. In our culture, it is considered unwise to move when twins are very young. People believe that if you move too quickly after the birth of twins, one of them will surely die. We'll just have to wait until he and his wife decide it will be safe to move the babies."

So we waited. After four months, the man finally brought his family into their new home.

The twentieth house we completed also sat vacant for months. Others told me it was because the family did not have furniture. By this time I had learned it was no use to struggle with the people. They would move in when they resolved their particular problem and not before. I never spoke to that family about the matter and five months later they moved in.

These cases were not the rule. Almost all the families couldn't wait to move in. The fact that they had no curtains or furniture, or that the house was not finished, made no difference. They just wanted to get out of their shack and into that new home.

Monthly payments on the houses began before the houses were completed. Hence, the fact that a family did not move in had no effect on these payments. The procedure was that once we were well along in the construction of a group of houses, we would inaugurate the monthly payments for the entire group at the same time. The families did not object to this, for they were anxious to start liquidating their debt. Starting the payments a bit early was also a tremendous help to the project, since it returned money more quickly to the Fund for Humanity to help build more houses.

The monthly payments were based on the cost of the house. These costs were calculated somewhat in accordance with the scriptural injunction not to let your left hand know what your right hand does. Our "right hand" in the construction work was the Block and Sand Project. When the "left hand" was calculating the cost of the houses, we "didn't know" that the Block and Sand Project made hundreds of trips to the construction site to bring over the sand, blocks and cement. Neither did we "know" that we hired workers for many weeks to open up the streets in the project and ran the Block and Sand Project dump truck for hundreds of miles hauling in fill dirt for these streets.

In calculating the housing costs we considered not only the price of nails, wood, cement and tin, but we remembered also that this was God's project and that we were building for His needy people. We had our eyes on them, and we were keenly aware of their meager incomes as we figured the price on each house. At the same time, the cost we arrived at was not totally unrelated to the actual cost. We simply did not count every cost, as a profit motivated enterprise would have done.

Once we established the cost of a house, we subtracted from it the amount of the down payment (usually Z100) and divided the balance by 240 (the number of months in 20 years) to get the monthly payment. No interest was added. This was a key feature in the plan. Without interest, the payments were low enough to be met by a poor family and still leave enough money to live on. If we added interest, the families simply could not have made the payments.

Consider a typical example: The smallest three-bedroom house cost $1,060 to build. Without interest, the monthly payment amounted to $4.00. The family who was to live in the house had a monthly income of $25.00 to support the husband and wife, their five children, a brother of the husband, an aunt of the wife, and two children of the wife's brother living in the interior who sent the children to the city to attend school. Even the $4.00 payment was a big bite out of this meager income.

But what if 10 per cent interest (a very conservative figure in Zaire) was added to the payment? It jumped from $4.00 to $12.00 a month. That was slightly less than half the total income of the family, and there was no way they could pay it. Thus any kind of conventional financing of houses for poor families was impractical. If their miserable situation was to be alleviated, some Fund for Humanity type of philosophy had to be involved.

Initial costs and monthly payments on some of the other houses we built were:

> four-bedroom cost $1,780; monthly payment $7.00,
> five-bedroom cost $2,068; monthly payment $8.20,
> six-bedroom cost $2,308; monthly payment $9.20.

Families for Bokotola were selected by the Management Committee of the Fund for Humanity. Initially, this committee consisted of Pastor Boyaka, bishop of the church; Pastor Mpombo, auxiliary bishop; Ikete, projects director of the church, and myself. In 1976, Larry Stoner replaced me on the committee. Selections were made from the 3,000-plus applications that we had on file.

In these selections and in the management of the housing project itself, we were guided by seven principles that we established at our first meeting. These principles were:

1. *Houses will be built only for families who do not presently have adequate housing and who do not have the financial means to build.*

This principle was of primary importance for two reasons:

First, there were some families who had a good house or houses, and who simply wanted to take advantage of a good deal in order to get another house.

I recall one occasion, soon after the launching of the housing project, when a distinguished Zairois called me to his house. He was the director of an important government office in the city. When I arrived, he came right to the point.

"I want one of those houses you are building," he said.

I laughed and answered in a lighthearted way, "But I see you already have a very nice house."

"Yes," he replied, "and I have three more, too, but I want you to build me a fifth one!"

I explained the philosophy of the program, and I concluded by telling him that he could not possibly qualify for a house. He was not happy to hear this, and he continued to argue with me for several minutes. Finally I excused myself and left him grumbling.

We could have selected people of Mbandaka at random, and over 90 per cent of them would have qualified as living in inadequate housing. Clearly, however, this gentleman was not one of them.

Second, there was a need to establish who did qualify for a house. We chose the term "adequate housing" rather than some arbitrary rule such as, "someone whose house is made of mud," or "someone who lives in a house of less than three rooms," because a person who earned $150 a month could be worse off than someone who made $50 for a number of different reasons.

For example, one family was chosen for a house at Bokotola whose income was $150 a month, but the father of that family had *forty-five* people dependent on his income! That same father was in the process of building a good house, but over a four-year period he had not been able to save enough money to finish it. The committee decided that he merited a house, although he had a larger income than most, and eventually he would have two houses. For forty-five people, two houses would not be too many!

Furthermore, a great many people in Mbandaka owned their own homes. Land was not expensive; a few dollars would buy a small lot. On this lot, a mud shack was built and covered with palm branches. This made the person a homeowner, but should that mud shack disqualify him from a house at Bokotola? Obviously not.

By the same token, there were some families living in houses made of durable materials, but either the accommodations were much too small for the size of the family, or they were rented, or some other problem made them inadequate.

In addition, although we wanted to exclude those who had resources to build their own homes, we did not want to choose families for Bokotola solely from the bottom rung of the economic ladder. Within the criterion of "lacking adequate housing" we tried to select a group of families representing various levels of advancement and income. We wanted to build a viable community, not a ghetto.

2. *Families chosen to have houses must pay $100 or more as a down payment.*

The second principle was also established for two reasons:

First, there were thousands of families in need of housing in the city. We felt that those families who had made the effort to save enough money for a down payment should be preferred over those who had not, since it was impossible to build a house for everybody who needed one.

Second, we had to have this contribution from the families to help with the Fund for Humanity!

3. *Only families with a good reputation for honesty will be chosen—that is to say, only families who, it is believed, will regularly make the required monthly payments.*

This principle was established because we felt that if we had two groups of poor people, one honest and one dishonest, we should prefer the honest ones! As Christians we should not be against a decent place to live for dishonest people, but since we didn't have enough resources to help everybody, we felt justified in preferring the honest folk (or people the committee believed would be reliable in making the required payments). The long-range future of the venture would largely depend on these payments, and that made this principle doubly important.

4. *All houses will be built on the land known as Bokotola, the land granted to the church by the Zaire Government.*

This rule was necessary because literally hundreds of people came to us requesting that we build houses on their lots. We knew that if we did that, we couldn't control and supervise the work. Neither could we build the community in the name of Christ which the church was struggling to establish.

We did make one exception to this principle, however, when we built a small house in the city for an old crippled pastor. This was a result of a special Christmas Day program in 1975.

The Zaire Government had eliminated Christmas as an official holiday. Work, school, and all other workday activities were to go on as usual. The president of Zaire had explained this by saying, "Christ was born at midnight. If you want to celebrate his birth, do it at midnight. Work on Christmas Day instead of going out and getting drunk."

Since Christmas would be a workday, we decided to make it a very special one. Early on Christmas morning all of our sixty workers from the construction site and the Block and Sand Project met in the community building at Bokotola. We had special singing groups, Bible readings, prayer, and a meditation. The Scripture readings and talk were on the theme of Jesus' birth and the significance of His coming into the world.

I spoke about Christ's command that we love our neighbors and His teaching that our neighbor is anyone, anywhere, who needs us. I told the story of the Good Samaritan, using the device of a man going from Bolenge to Mbandaka. A local pastor passed by on the other side, too busy to help. So did a local businessman. Then an Angolan refugee stopped and took the man to the hospital. I concluded by saying that God calls us to help those in need, regardless of race or tribal affiliation.

After the meditation, we gave each worker the equivalent of one dollar along with these instructions: "Jesus told us to love our neighbor as we love ourselves. Therefore, you may use half the money for yourself and use the other half to help someone in need. Find someone who will be surprised at your generosity and your offer to help, someone who is not a family member or close friend who would be expecting your help; share your money with that person or family, and work for them today. Consider the *whole day* as a worship service, not just that portion here in the community building. Today you will be working for God, and you are only responsible to Him. The service will end tomorrow morning when you come back and tell us how you spent Christmas Day."

Finally, each worker was given two colorful tracts in the Lingala language on the birth of Jesus—one for himself and one for the person he worked for. Then we dismissed the men, and they went out into the city.

The morning following Christmas Day we gathered for the conclusion of the Christmas service. The men were obviously excited. When they started telling of their experiences, they were so worked up they all wanted to talk at the same time. They had found real joy as they went about helping others in Christ's name. Some had cut wood for old people. Others had assisted people on the roads who were carrying heavy loads. One man sorrowfully helped a neighbor bury his child. Others bought food and medicines for the old and the sick. At the close everyone decided spontaneously to make the program an annual occasion.

Six of us chose to begin Pastor Balusu's house as our Christmas Day work. There were five workers who accompanied me to the home of Balusu, the old crippled pastor whom I had met a few weeks earlier when a younger pastor had taken me to visit. He lived alone in a mud shack that was at the point of total collapse. Inside the shack were several hundred concrete blocks he had been saving for twelve years in hopes of one day building a new house. But now he was too old and crippled to work, and his income consisted only of a pension of $10 a month. His wife was dead, and his only child, a daughter, was married and lived in a distant village. All he could do was to buy enough food to stay alive—there was absolutely no way he could build a better house.

We plunged in as fast as we could to dig the foundation and then pour it, with his neighbors beginning to get caught up in the spirit of the effort and coming to help. One woman stood at the well for two hours just drawing water to mix the cement. When the foundation was finished, just before dark, we stood around in the front yard and talked about what we had done and why. Sharing a song and a closing prayer climaxed a beautiful experience, surely the most meaningful Christmas I have ever spent.

A few weeks later, some men from the Bokotola work crew, along with Joe, Ken and Larry, returned to finish the job. On the day Pastor Balusu moved in, he sighed that he was "like a slave in that old house, but now through God's love I have been set free."

5. *Only one house may be built on each lot. Additions or other buildings are prohibited except as approved by the committee in writing.*

This was an attempt to avoid the development of a slum area, and to preserve the aesthetics of the community. We had made the lots deliberately large in order to give open space between the houses and to enable the families to plant gardens or keep chickens. But these advantages would be lost if people started indiscriminately building other dwelling shacks. Interestingly enough, residents enthusiastically endorsed this idea, feeling that they would be protected from these undesired developments since the prohibitions applied to all.

6. *The beneficiaries of the houses are invited to contribute to the Fund for Humanity in a spontaneous manner.*

This rule was established in hopes of drawing people into

the spirit of the Fund for Humanity. In terms of contributing money, this did not happen. Some of the people donated their labor from time to time to help push the work along, but even that help was not really significant except when they were working on their own lots. We did not find much community spirit in terms of helping others outside the family. It is true that the people are very poor and that not much could be expected, but this lack of expressed concern for others was still a disappointment.

7. *Families are encouraged to assist in the construction of their houses by their manual labor (clearing the lots, etc.).*

The last principle was, by and large, observed quite well. People were so happy to be getting a house that they tended to work on their lot every chance they got. On many afternoons, especially immediately after a new group of families had been chosen, there would be literally scores of men, women and children up and down the streets, all industriously cleaning off their newly-assigned properties.

In addition to following the written principles, the committee tried to select people from many walks of life. We chose pastors and laymen, Protestants and Catholics, government workers, truck drivers, nurses, shop clerks, mechanics, tailors, young people, and retired folk. And we chose several women. Normally, the man is the head of the household in Zaire, and if a family exists, the man holds title to any real estate it may own. If this man dies, however, he leaves his property to a brother or to a son, and only rarely does he leave real property to his wife. Thus a widow or a divorced woman is almost always left without a house, even though her husband may·have had one. There are also many unmarried women with children in Zairois society. Women in all of these categories were granted houses at Bokotola.

Most of the families chosen were monogamous, but a few men had more than one wife. One man had four, but only one of his wives had borne children. Another man, with only one tiny wife, had sixteen children, with the oldest being sixteen years old! Some of the children were twins, however.

As the project grew, many people came to help on a volunteer basis. We always told them that they were free to work— we needed all the help we could get—but their work would not assure them a house. In practice, we did give preference to people who had worked faithfully as volunteers, if they qualified according to the seven principles. Some of the higher-income people in town hired people to work in their place at the project, but when we made it clear they would not get a house because they didn't qualify under the rules, they became suddenly uninterested in charity. One man, an official in the central prison, sent over a group of prisoners to work on his behalf, but we refused to accept their labor, knowing the man was only trying to use them for his own selfish interests. The selection process was a grueling one, and final decisions were often agonizing. In addition to the thousands of written applications, hordes of individual candidates wanted to talk personally to me and to the other committee members, especially the chairman, Pastor Boyaka. On some days a dozen people would be crowded around the door of our home. At the church headquarters there would be a large crowd sitting outside the door of Pastor Boyaka's office. Most of the people were polite in asking, but there were those who were not. Some could be unbelievably insistent.

Here is a typical exchange between an applicant and myself:

CITIZEN: I'm here to see about the question of getting a house at Bokotola. I sent in my letter of request six months ago and I haven't received a reply.

M.F.: Citoyen, we have received thousands of request letters. It is impossible to answer all of them. We only reply to those who are selected.

CITIZEN: But you don't understand! I live in a terrible house. I've got nine children and we are suffering.

M.F.: Yes, I do understand. I wish we could build a house for every family that needs one in the entire city, but we cannot. We don't have the money. We are doing the best we can.

CITIZEN: But I need a house. My family is suffering.

(And on and on it would go. I would try in vain to explain that every application would be considered by the committee, but finally I would just have to walk away.)

Others used the attack-accusation tactic:

CITIZEN: Monsieur Fuller, why are you giving out the houses only to people who already have lots of houses instead of to people who really need them?

M.F.: Who has received a house at Bokotola who already has other houses?

CITIZEN: There have been several.

M.F.: Who?

CITIZEN: Oh, I don't want to name them.

(At that point I would pull out the list of people who had been chosen to that point and start calling off names.)

M.F.: Lokesa. Do you know him?

CITIZEN: Yes.

M.F.: Does he have other houses?

CITIZEN: No.

M.F.: Ilanga. Do you know him?
CITIZEN: Yes.
M.F.: Does he have other houses?
CITIZEN: No.
M.F.: Bolembe. Do you know him?
CITIZEN: No.
M.F.: Well, he is a chauffeur and he makes Z18 a month. Do you think he is a rich man with lots of houses?
CITIZEN: No.

(Thus I would continue down the list, to the mounting embarrassment of the accuser, until he withdrew that particular argument.)

One day as I was working at my desk I heard a vehicle roll up outside; then the horn blew. Since I was very busy I ignored it, feeling that if there was some good reason the person needed to see me he could walk to the door and knock.

After a minute or so I heard the door of the vehicle open and then slam shut. A moment later I heard the living-room door open and someone stomped through the house toward the room where I was working. A well-dressed young Zairois man entered.

"*Bonjour,*" he said, as he tossed a letter in front of me.

He spread his legs apart, crossed his arms and silently waited for me to read the letter. It was a note from a Belgian acquaintance of mine simply stating that he knew this fellow and that he wanted a house at Bokotola.

"You want a house at Bokotola, I see."

"Yes," he said.

"But you look to be a person with money. Bokotola is a project for poor people."

He put on a big smile. "No, I'm a very poor person. You can't pay any attention to these clothes!"

"Where do you live?" I asked. He named a place I hadn't heard of. "Where is that?"

"It's about 100 kilometers from here."

"Well, I don't see how you would qualify for a house here since we only build for people who live in Mbandaka."

"Oh, but I want to move here as soon as you get my house built."

"Well, the procedure is for you to write a request letter to the president of the Selection Committee, Pastor Boyaka Inkomo, and we will consider it in committee meeting, but I should tell you that you will probably not be selected, because you do not live in Mbandaka. And, also, your request is a bit late, since we have already received and recorded over 3,000 requests."

"But you can intervene for me?"

"How can I intervene for you? I don't know you. You just came stalking in the house a few minutes ago."

"But you've got the letter from *le blanc* (the white man)."

"That letter simply says you want to talk to me about a house. If he wants to write you a letter of recommendation to go along with your letter he can do that."

"Why can't you write such a letter?"

"I don't know you."

"You mean you are going to leave me just like that? I come in here with this letter and you give me an answer like that?"

"What do you mean? I don't understand."

"I mean, you are not going to help me get a house even though I came with that letter?"

"No. I've explained the procedure. Write a letter making a formal request. Include a letter from your friend if he will write one. I can't do anything else for you."

"Humph!" He grabbed up the letter from in front of me and stormed out of the house. I never heard from him again.

After we set the date for each meeting to select families, members of the committee would go through the file of request letters and pull out a number of candidates to be considered. These candidates would be given to me or Ikete or Larry Stoner. Then, a couple of weeks before the meeting, we would start our investigations. We rode all over the city, bouncing across huge mudholes and ditches, to visit hundreds of families.

On Selection Day we opened the meeting with a time of prayer; then we gave our eyewitness reports, and the difficult process began. We considered each candidate, and then started the painful elimination process. Usually, we chose at least one workman from the Block and Sand Project and one from the construction crew, plus some of the volunteers. When all the selections were finally made, Pastor Boyaka would announce, "Go, and close your ears!" He knew, as we all did, that there would be a few very happy people, and many more not at all happy. There would be criticism and accusations, but we had done the best we could.

Immediately after each group of families was chosen, a meeting was held with them to explain the seven principles and the philosophy of the Fund for Humanity, and to answer their questions. A second meeting was called after all the houses in the group were well along in construction. Both sessions were held in the community building and were marked by joyous singing and preaching.

At the second meeting, we were ready to explain the agreement and have it signed by all parties. Ikete, as projects director, read the agreement line by line in French and then gave a translation in Lingala, allowing time for questions after the reading of each article.

The official contract consisted of twelve articles which stated as simply as possible the items to be agreed upon between the church, as the Seller, and each family, as the Buyer. These items included:

a. A clear listing of the purchase price, the down payment already made, the amount of each monthly payment, and the possible penalties for lateness. Final recourse in the event of default, after all other negotiations had failed, would be eviction of the Buyer, in which case ownership would revert automatically to the church.

b. The prohibition of any other construction or addition on the Buyer's lot without written approval from the church.

c. A statement of the Buyer's obligation to keep the house, lot, and drainage ditch in good condition and to cooperate with other residents in caring for the park area.

d. The naming of a specific person to take possession of the house and fulfill all the obligations of ownership in the event of the Buyer's death.

After all questions of rights and responsibilities under the terms of the contract had been discussed, each family was called separately to a table in the center of the room to sign the agreement in front of witnesses.

Following this signing ceremony the "payments annex" was explained. This annex included neat little blocks for all 240 months of the twenty-year payment period, so that as payments were made they could be noted in the appropriate square.

We strongly encouraged families to pay more than the required monthly payment whenever they could, for two reasons: *First*, they could get a little ahead as a form of insurance in case they lost their job, became ill, or had some other unexpected expense. They could afford to miss a few payments at that time if they had paid in advance. *Second*, they would be returning extra money to the Fund for Humanity which could be put to work immediately to build more houses for more needy families.

Both the contract and the payments annex were made out in duplicate. The original of each went to the office of the Treasurer of the church, and the copy to the owner. The owner took the copy each time he went to make a payment, and the Treasurer placed the copy under the original with a piece of carbon paper between so that what he wrote on the original would also be recorded on the copy. In this way there would never be any question about what had been paid. Also, the owner would always have in his hands an easily understandable record of how much he had paid and what he still owed on his house.

There were doubters, of course, who insisted the people would not fulfill their obligations: "They will pay for a while, but then they will stop making the payments." This could happen, but I am optimistic that it will not. The rights and obligations are clearly spelled out in writing; everyone knows exactly what is required of him. The procedures are well established and have been in the hands of local church authorities from the very first day. It is up to them, of course, to ensure compliance; I think they will, because they are eager for the venture to be a continuing success. Furthermore, the payments are reasonable and within the means of the families. They got a "good deal," and they know this, and they appreciate what they have received. All of these factors combine to make me an optimist about Bokotola.

By mid-1976 there were some families behind in their payments, but no one family was more than three months in arrears. Several occupants had paid one or two months in advance; one was six months ahead. The total paid up to that date amounted to more than the required payments. In other words, considering all the families together, they had paid in advance rather than falling in arrears. I believe this trend will continue, and one day, with their obligations completed, these families will be able to say thankfully *"Ndako na ngai* (my house)" and mean it 100 per cent!

14

Losanganya

AS the end of our three-year tour in Zaire approached, the pace of activities became really hectic. On the one hand life continued fairly normally, with about one equipment break-down or similar episode per day. On the other hand the whole family was sorting and organizing, packing and discarding, attending end-of-term school exercises along with an incredible assortment of farewell conclaves and feasts. The sadness of separation from so many wonderful friends was mixed with celebrations of joy for the relationships we had shared.

One of the most memorable of these occasions required an overnight trip to Mbomba's home village, about 150 miles south of Mbandaka. Mbomba and his relatives had planned a full day of festivities, including speechmaking, women's synchronized dancing, the presentation of gifts, and of course a colossal *"au revoir"* feast.

At one point a collection of large drums was set up in the center of the village for a joyous time of dancing. After watching a while I decided to jump into the circle and dance too, and the townspeople went wild. They were shrieking, bouncing up and down, bending double with laughter, slapping each other on the back, pointing and yelling. It was obviously the first time a white man had joined in their dances!

Then I began calling the old women of the village, one at a time, to come and dance with me. They beamed and acquiesced, giggling like a bunch of teen-agers, while the onlookers roared even louder. This jubilant exercise continued for over an hour, and I stored up yet another unforgettable experience to take home.

All our activities during those final weeks were pointed toward July 4, 1976. Americans elsewhere were celebrating their country's bicentennial, but the notable event in Mbandaka on that date was the grand dedication service at Bokotola.

On the great day people began arriving early. Eventually they filled every space in the community building and were spilling out in all directions into the park and adjoining streets. There were delegates to the annual General Assembly of the Church of Equator Region just opening in Mbandaka, along with other Protestant leaders from a wide area; representatives of the Catholic church; members of the one hundred families who had been chosen for houses in Bokotola; prominent businessmen, both Zairois and foreign, along with local and regional Government dignitaries, including the Governor of Equator Region representing President Mobutu. Also, there were a great many other interested people who wanted to share in the excitement of this occasion.

Palm branches lined the freshly swept streets and encircled the park. Banners and gigantic Zairois flags waved overhead. Special singing groups were at the center of the throng, dressed in colorful African prints. They began to hum a soft background, gently thumping their drums and rattling their shakers.

When everyone was in place Ikete stood, motioning for all to join him, and in enthusiastic unison the crowd raised the Zairois national anthem. Then Pastor Boyaka Inkomo, regional bishop of the Disciples Community, delivered the official welcoming speech, and found it "a most agreeable duty."

Re-emphasizing the call of the gospel to minister to the total man, to meet both his spiritual and material needs, Pastor Boyaka stated that the church's involvement in Bokotola was "on orders from our Master, who said to help our neighbor." He went on to outline the history of the venture, detailing the procedures followed in choosing families. Then everyone who had contributed to the project was thanked specifically, beginning with all of us who worked locally, continuing to President Mobutu, and finally reaching the supporting churches, organizations, and individuals overseas.

His conclusion contained a new proposal, carefully prepared for this dedication service.

To form a prosperous and unified community of people coming from different tribes and from different religious confessions; to break down the barriers which separate the whites from the blacks; to form a society which knows no sort of discrimination—that is the aim of the Fund for Humanity.

Therefore we now propose to the authorities of the Sub-Region to change the name of *Bokotola*, which signifies "the person who does not like others," to *Losanganya*, which means "reconciler, reunifier, everyone together." Furthermore, we propose to give this park where you are now gathered the official name of *Tosalisana*, meaning "let's love each other." From this day on, the spirit of our project in Mbandaka will be expressed to everyone who hears its name.

The crowd applauded enthusiastically, and it was done. The name of the new community officially became. Losanganya, symbolizing the bringing together of people, in the name of Christ, on the piece of land which had formerly kept them apart.

Then the Governor rose to respond:

I bring you the urgent revolutionary greetings of the father of the nation, Citizen Mobutu Sese Seko Kuku Ngbendu Wa Za Banga, President Founder of the Popular Revolutionary Movement and President of the Republic ...

The construction of houses in favor of those who are in need is not only the business of Mobutu but of everyone of good will. That is what the Church of Christ of Zaire has understood so well. ... The realization of this most beautiful section of the city is the fruit of the good will of foreigners and local people working together ...

May all foreigners from far or near who contributed to this project find here the expression of our profound revolutionary gratitude. May they be assured that their names will remain engraved in golden letters in the annals of the city of Mbandaka ...

The government is disposed to cooperate with the church in its efforts and to grant to it more land to intensify the program. The requests for houses, which now exceed four thousand, suggest that the program ought to be expanded to build four thousand houses!

The project of Losanganya ought to serve as a model to precipitate a revolution of benevolence concerning lodging. ... We wait to see a continuation of this program ... bringing a better life to all the people of Zaire.

Now Mama Beyeke and her singing group moved to the center of the crowd. Starting slowly, they built up to a smiling, pounding, rattling, shaking cacophony of sounds. With Mama Beyeke leading, the chorus sang about what Pastor Boyaka and the Governor had said. The people were admonished to follow the speakers' good advice, and the listeners roared approval.

Then the musicians sang about the *mundeles* who had been coming to help and urged the people to love and protect them. The audience whistled, stamped, and cheered. There was a steady crescendo in the singing even as the tempo grew wilder and faster. Mama Beyeke lifted her hands in the air as she jerked her head from side to side in the intensity of her performance.

Suddenly, her hands came straight down to her sides, and the spectacle abruptly ended. The crowd exploded in shouts of appreciation.

When the excitement died down, Ikete asked everyone to stand and led them in a rousing rendition of "What a Friend

We Have in Jesus." Then the audience settled back in quiet expectancy as Dr. Bokeleale, president of the Church of Christ of Zaire, moved to the podium to deliver the dedication sermon. Some of the thoughts in his long address will always stay with me.

Bokotola-Losanganya is a witness, a sermon, a prophecy, pushing all of us to think of others. It gives flesh and blood to the church's proclamation of concern and love for God's people in need ...

But when I see this project being fulfilled, I am sad, distressed. I am surprised that I feel like that. It is beautiful, one can rejoice. But if you are pleased, I am not. I am sad because I know the possibility to do more than this ...

In America and here, everywhere, we can build houses like these. The strong of this world have not understood their responsibility. When the gospel speaks of the strong supporting the weak, there are two ideas presented. First, if you are strong in your faith, you must seek out others, to make their faith stronger. This support suggests a vertical direction. But there is also a horizontal direction. That is to say, the gospel is concerned with the great physical needs of our brothers, and here the strong also must support the weak.

I told you I am not satisfied ... I am even sad. ... In some ways we have weakened the church in doing this project. Why? Because there has been anger, jealousy, and resentment in the hearts of many people. Everyone was hungry, and there was food to eat, but it wasn't sufficient. There are now nearly *five thousand* requests for houses; there are only 162 houses.

Brother Fuller, that is the message you must take to America. God sent you here to Zaire. I know you were a lawyer in America, and I know how well American lawyers live. I have seen their homes. Big houses—few people in them. It is scandalous. ... I am not an economist; I am a pastor. But I understand that in the world where we live more than half of all the riches are in one single country.

We are in an area peopled by the Bantu. Our ancestors were never against the rich—they always wished to have wealthy people among them. They said a village with no wealthy people was a dead village. But they also said one is not rich only for himself, but he is rich for others as well. There are individuals in America who could donate five million dollars. If one person would give this to Mr. Fuller, no one can imagine how many houses we could build in Mbandaka!

Our ancestors have another proverb. If a bird is tied up, he will peck at his bonds with his bill. Little by little he will peck at the cords holding him, and finally he is free. We Zairois cannot wait for outsiders to come and do all things for us. We have the responsibility to organize ourselves and little by little to use our own bills to liberate ourselves from the situations which bind us.

When I was at the Bolenge Seminary as a young man a pastor provoked me with a sermon. He said that the God we love has no hands. I had a concept of God with a long beard, somewhat like an old man of my village. I couldn't understand his image.

Then he explained: "We are the hands of God."
I see young Americans here working with this project. I see local people, too, contributing here. And I see another American, an old man like me who is here giving of himself. Here, God's hands are at work.
But not everywhere. This is why I am not satisfied—I know the enormous possibilities. ...
May the venture of Bokotola-Losanganya be just the beginning of a glorious day of working together in Christ's name to minister to the suffering and the weak. And may the Savior pardon us all and help us in this task.

"Ummmmmmmm," the people sighed their approval. And the service closed with more joyful music and the distribution of Lingala Bibles to each of the families in the new development of Losanganya.

The project had been started just two years earlier. In that time we had cleared the land, put in the permanent boundary markers, and begun construction on all 114 houses in the original plot. Eighty families were now making their monthly payments into the Fund for Humanity, and hundreds of people were already living in the community.
The park area was completely developed, including the modern community building, imaginative play equipment for children, a soccer field, sand pit, and the unique "women's foyer." Mbomba's furniture shop was running smoothly, turning out doors, windows, chairs, beds, desks, tables, and other furniture of good quality. The community clinic was in operation. Many families were cultivating productive gardens on their plots.
Management of the continuing development of Losanganya was left with Ikete, as projects director, and Larry Stoner. The day-to-day supervision of the workmen was in the hands of Mbomba, our capable and conscientious foreman. Also Dale Long, a new volunteer from the Mennonite Central Committee, had arrived in June to work entirely in community development—to launch more "backyard industries," plant more gardens, and organize other self-help programs.
Prospects for completing the development, including forty-eight more houses and a second community park, appeared excellent. At the time of our departure, income for the Fund for Humanity from house payments totaled $750 a month. The Block and Sand Project was consistently producing $1,000 a month profit, all of which went into the Fund for Humanity. Many friends from overseas who had helped from the very beginning had pledged continuing support. The Congrega-

tional Church in Plymouth, New Hampshire, which had paid
for the first house in the community, pledged to pay for the one
hundredth as well!

Local interest and support was growing. At the dedication
service the Mbandaka Lions Club (yes, there is one—its members are largely foreign and Zairois businessmen and local
government leaders) announced its decision to finance the development of the second community park. Three months earlier they had made their first contribution, which had paid for
the foundation of the community building. And more and more
local volunteers were appearing, carrying blocks for the masons, mixing cement, opening new roads in the extension, and
assisting in countless other ways.

As our family flew out of Mbandaka on the day after the
dedication service, we looked down on the glistening roofs of
Losanganya spread out below us. It was a beautiful sight, and
we were thrilled to see this panoramic view of a dream un-
folded into sparkling reality. We believe, however, that we
were seeing not only one dream realized, but also the beginning of another.

15

On to Ntondo

WHEN we left Zaire in July of 1976 we were confident that the new development, now called Losanganya, would be finished. But we were even more excited to know that the experiment at Losanganya was more than a one-time project. We had discovered a way of building which could be duplicated in many needy communities.

At the beginning of the year Dr. Bokeleale had written a letter of appreciation for the growth that was taking place in the new community, at the same time urging us to try to widen the effort.

"It is really a miracle," he wrote, "to see the fine buildings and the help you are bringing to families who never had the slightest hope of possessing a decent home. ... The project simply must be enlarged. The experience has been so worthwhile that we must see how it can be extended elsewhere in our country."

A few weeks later I received a visit from Mompongo Mo Imana, a close Zairois friend. He arrived at our home early one evening, and after an exchange of pleasant greetings he came right to the point.

"Millard, I want to talk to you about the possibility of doing a Bokotola-like project in my village of Ntondo."

I was immediately interested, because Mompongo is an extraordinary fellow. I did not know of any other person in whom I would have more confidence to lead a follow-up program. Educated in the United States (he speaks nearly flawless English), he is one of those rare Africans who returned to his home in the interior to help his people.

Ntondo is a small village of some three thousand people, situated on the eastern edge of Lake Tumba, about ninety miles south of Mbandaka. Its inhabitants survive on subsistence farming, and by fishing in the huge lake. A few also raise cocoa and coffee on small farms, and many of the women prepare *kwanga* to sell in the markets of Mbandaka.

When Mompongo came back to the village following his university training, he plunged into the task of building a modern high school for the village and surrounding area. He simply organized the people into work teams and started in. Little by little, working with rudimentary equipment and whatever money could be raised locally, plus gifts he obtained from friends back at his alma mater, Washington State University in Pullman, he built his high school. It took eight years, but the finished structure is a beautiful, spacious building for 700 students. Mompongo became the first director, and classes began years before the structure was completed, with students contributing labor to finish the job.

The school has become widely known, not only for its impressive building, but also for the quality of its program. Dormitories have been built, and boarding students come from hundreds of miles around. In addition to developing this big secondary school, Mompongo coordinated simultaneously the building of *six* junior high schools in surrounding villages to feed students into the high school.

When we arrived in Equator Region in 1973, Mompongo was still director of the Ntondo high school, but his extraordinary accomplishments had already come to the attention of Zaire Government authorities, and they had offered him a high position in school administration. He had resisted this effort at first, but finally in 1975 accepted the post of head of the Education Department for Equator Region. He and his family then moved to Mbandaka, the capital of the Region. When he was being sought after by the Government, he stipulated that he wanted to stay in Equator Region in order to pursue his dream of developing his home village. He saw the building of the school as only the beginning.

Linda and I had traveled to Ntondo several times. We enjoyed visiting Mompongo and the British Baptist missionaries who worked there. Our visits, always on week ends, included sharing in the worship service of the village church. Mompongo was a leader in that congregation as Sunday school teacher, pianist, and sometime preacher.

Now Mompongo was ready for a new venture.

"Millard, this is something I want to do. I've watched the unfolding of Bokotola, and it has been an inspiration. But even before you started that project I was wondering how we could get our people in Ntondo out of those miserable shacks and into better houses. The school was a start, but now we need to take the next step. Our people are energetic and open to new

things. I know that if we proposed such a project in Ntondo
there would be immediate acceptance and everyone would
work wholeheartedly with us."

"But, Mompongo, you live here now. How could you give
leadership to such an undertaking, living in Mbandaka and
charged with the heavy responsibilities of your office?"

"I can do it. As you know, the roads down to Ntondo are
much better now, and I can make the trip in three to four
hours. Also, I know several people in the village who will
share this responsibility—men who are hardworking and capable...and honest. My heart is down there, and I am thoroughly
committed to this effort. But we cannot do the job alone. We
are poor and must have outside help—people to work with us,
and money to buy materials." ... We talked until nearly
midnight.

The following night we got together again, this time with
Larry, Ken, Joe, Chuck and Cindy. This second meeting also
lasted several hours, and we became more and more excited as
we listened to Mompongo spell out his dream, and his willingness to pour himself into the effort. At the conclusion of this
session, we decided the next step was to go to the village and
call a mass meeting to get the reaction of the people.

The following week end, everyone from this meeting except
myself went down to Ntondo. On Sunday night, the six of
them fairly burst into our living room.

"Millard, you wouldn't have believed how excited those people were!" Larry exclaimed. "We had practically nonstop
meetings from Saturday afternoon until noon today, and the
people were so turned on! I can't get over it! Man, do they
ever want this thing!"

Joe chimed in, "Yes. They obviously respect Mompongo,
and they'll follow his leadership. We'll have even more community participation there than we've experienced here in
Mbandaka."

They went on to tell me that the church had officially voted
to establish the Ntondo Fund for Humanity to launch the
housing-community development program. The Management
Committee had been elected, with Mompongo as coordinator,
the amount of the down payment established at eighty Zaires,
and families invited to start making down payments to the
newly-elected treasurer. Before our crew had left Ntondo, six
families had already paid!

It had been decided earlier that we would not use a selection procedure at Ntondo as we had in Mbandaka. There were only about three hundred families in the village, and all of them were poor. We would tackle the job of building houses for *everybody*. We would accept the exciting challenge of total community development—including homes for all the families, well-planned streets, garden areas, parks, small industries and community enrichment activities.

It had also been decided that even though the houses should be as large as the Mbandaka houses (because the families were equally large), we would cut out several things in order to keep the payments lower. (Family incomes in this village were considerably lower than in Mbandaka.) We would have no interior doors, no ceilings, no paint, and windows with wooden panels instead of glass panes. In short, the structures would be "shell" houses onto which doors, ceilings, paint, and windows could be added as the occupants could afford them. In the meantime, families could be living in a decent house that did not leak and that kept them off the damp earth, at a monthly payment they could meet without depriving themselves of other necessities.

We wanted to begin surveying for the project immediately, but Chuck, our surveyor, was about to leave for the States. The committee decided to continue to accept down payments, and to have the people start hauling sand and gravel from the lake so that a big stockpile would be available whenever a surveyor could be found.

Within a few months the treasurer had received down payments of nearly two thousand Zaires; Ken Sauder had requested and received from the Mennonite Central Committee a transfer to work full time at Ntondo; and back at Koinonia we found our surveyor. Ryan Karis, a Quaker from Marshall, Indiana, and his wife Karen, a Lutheran from Livingston, Montana, had first met when both came as volunteers to Koinonia in 1973. Now he was in charge of the home-building crew, and Karen headed the pecan-shipping department. They decided together to take a leave to do the survey work at Ntondo; Karen would also teach English classes at the high school and work with the women of the community. In November of 1976 the Division of Overseas Ministries of the Disciples Church agreed to sponsor them for this project.

Shortly before our family left Zaire we had a visitor from the Department of Development of the church's national office in Kinshasa. He wanted to see the Ntondo site. I had also been planning to go, to meet personally with the Management Committee and to talk to the people of the village. Also, I needed to take photographs to use in soliciting help back in the States.

A trip was soon arranged. Mompongo would go down on a Sunday to prepare for our visit, and we would follow on Tuesday with Ken Sauder.

When we rolled into the village on Tuesday morning, we could immediately sense the excitement. A host of people fell in behind the Land Rover and ran after us. As we pulled into the yard of Mompongo's house (currently occupied by a teacher at the high school), someone started ringing the church bell. More people poured out of their houses and ran to greet us. Soon we were completely surrounded by a sea of smiling faces and dozens of hands reaching out for us to shake.

We chatted in the yard for a few minutes and then began walking through the village to the high school where, we had been told, Mompongo was meeting with the students. The people fell in behind us, and we created a grand procession down the main street. (This wide avenue, incidentally, is called "Melika," a corruption of the word *America*. It was given this name because of the ministry of American Baptist missionaries who came to Ntondo in the early 1900's. They turned the work over to the British Baptists in 1946.)

On and on we walked, picking up more marchers along the way. Then we turned off the main street and covered the remaining few hundred yards to the big high school. Classes were canceled in order to greet us, and hundreds of students poured out of the main entrance and crowded happily around us. Then, seeing the cameras, they wanted their pictures taken, so we spent a few minutes snapping photos.

From the school, we continued to a tour of the new dormitories, and then to the shore of the lake. The villagers had been digging sand and gravel and hauling it to the edge of the town in preparation for the construction work. They had been stocking this sand and gravel in three locations, and we were impressed to see how much had already been piled up, carried only in small baskets made from bark.

I congratulated the men on their efforts, but told them much more sand would be needed. Whereupon everyone answered at once: "We know, but we are not tired. We will continue. We will pile up a great quantity!"

At noon we had a special feast at the home of the new principal of the high school with the eight members of the

Management Committee. After the meal, the treasurer reported that he had in the Fund for Humanity the sum of Z2,320 paid in by twenty-nine families. Many other families, he said, were saving money for their down payment.

For over two hours we talked about the project: what kind of houses to build, how to determine priority in starting the houses (it was decided to build first for those families who were living in the very worst conditions), and where to begin construction.

One of the men raised a question about certain people, especially widows, who could neither raise the required down payment nor meet the monthly payments. After considerable discussion, it was decided that the Management Committee would consider these people on a case by case basis, and, if necessary, raise money through the church to help them. The committee was in full agreement that everybody in the village should have decent housing, and this meant building for all families except three, since only that small number already had a home constructed of durable materials.

At the conclusion of the session, we decided that the treasurer should give Mompongo Z1,600 from the treasury to order thirty tons of cement immediately. When this cement arrived, the people could start making and stockpiling blocks as they were already stockpiling sand and gravel. It was also decided that the villagers should begin making mud blocks right away with molds they already had—interior walls could be built with these less expensive blocks.

Clearing of undergrowth in the area chosen for the first construction would get under way immediately. We had concluded that it was possible to lay out a street in this area without a surveyor, since it closely followed the lakeside. We could also make a supply of concrete boundary markers in preparation for staking off the lots and streets when Ryan arrived.

We adjourned our planning session and headed toward the church for a mass meeting with the townspeople which was set for four o'clock. A crowd was already gathering as we walked up. The church bell was rung, and more throngs poured in until the building was packed and literally buzzing with excitement.

The leader of the church community, Pastor Nganda, started the meeting with several lively songs and a prayer. Then he turned the floor over to Mompongo who formally introduced each visitor, carefully explaining our roles in Mbandaka and Kinshasa. He went on to tell the purpose of our visit to Ntondo—to help realize their dream of developing their village. Then he beckoned me to come up.

"*Mbote!*" (Mmbo-tay) I shouted the traditional Lingala greeting to the expectant congregation.

"*Mmmbootaay!*" they thundered back.

"*Mbotay lesusu!*" (Hello again!) I shouted.

"*Mmmbootay!*" came back the reply even louder.

"*Mmbotay Mingi!*" (Hello a whole lot!) I thundered it out.

"*MMMMBOOOTAAY!*" The church fairly rattled as the people, in full voice by now, roared in unison their enthusiastic response.

"How many of you have seen the Mbandaka housing project?" I asked.

Hands went up all over the church. Possibly a third of the audience had been there.

"How many of you have heard others speak of that project?" Every hand went up.

"You know, then, that a project such as you propose for your village is possible. It is not easy, but it is possible. I remember well the day I went with the Mbandaka church leaders to see the Commissaire to request land for our Mbandaka project. After reading our proposal, he asked how much money we had. When I responded that we didn't have any, he asked how did we expect to build such a big project. I told him it was God's project, and that it is amazing how much He can do with very little. We explained our plans to get down payments, to ask friends in other countries to help us, and to use profits from the Block and Sand Project in the Fund for Humanity, but he was far from convinced. However, he decided to give us a tract of land, with the stipulation that if we had not started building within one year, the land would revert to the Government. A few weeks later, I received word from his office that he wanted to see me. When I walked in, he immediately challenged me.

" 'When are you going to start building those houses?'

" 'We've already started fifteen of them.'

" 'Fifteen! You've already started *fifteen* of them?' "

The people roared with laughter.

"You see," I went on, "that man doubted. He didn't know what God can do. When I think about the Ntondo project, I realize how little you have here, but as we start to build together we can take courage from an episode that took place one day in Jesus' ministry. He was outside a village, preaching to a big crowd that had gathered. He talked on and on, and the people were enthralled with his teaching.

"Night began to fall. The disciples came to Jesus and told him to send the people away so they could go back to the village and buy something to eat.

"Jesus responded, 'You give them something to eat.'

" 'But,' they said, 'we don't have anything. Only one little boy here has five loaves of bread and two little fish.'

" 'Bring them to me,' Jesus said.

"Then he took the bread and fish, gave thanks to God, and distributed the food to the people. And what happened? There was enough for everybody, with even some left over!

"You, the people of Ntondo, have little, and the task you seek to accomplish is enormous. You cannot possibly do the job by yourselves. But if you turn to God, asking Him to bless you and your venture, you will be amazed at what He can do with the little you have. Trust Him. Offer what you have, as the boy did. It might seem like a small amount, but if everyone contributes all that he can, you will succeed.

"Have faith in God; do not doubt; and give what you have. Others will help you, and you will not fail.

"God bless you as you work together in this venture of faith.

"*Mmbotay!*" I thundered out the Lingala greeting again.

"*MMMMBOOOTAAY!*" came back the reply, louder than ever.

After other words of encouragement and support from Ken, Pastor Nganda stood to respond.

"We thank God for this occasion," he began. "We thank God for what He is doing for Ntondo. We know what is happening comes from God, for we are no better than other villages. We are sinners and we disappoint God, but for some reason He has chosen to bless our village with this project, and we thank and praise Him.

"He has also chosen you, our visitors, to work with us. We thank God for you. And we want you to know that we feel so good about your friendship with us that we would like to swallow you—but we cannot because your shoulders are too big!"

As the meeting closed and the people poured out into the dusk, I felt close to the spirit of God. Along with Pastor Nganda, I knew that God had called us to Ntondo, and that we were embarking upon another exciting adventure of faith with Him.

16

New Frontiers

BEYOND Losanganya and Ntondo, what? Of course—another dream. This time the dream of a new organization, a center, to locate, inaugurate, and coordinate other housing and community projects in underdeveloped areas—in the United States as well as in other countries.

We intend to seek out and challenge more young people like Larry Stoner and our other volunteers to go forth to serve, and we must encourage older people to go as well. We want to become monumental beggars for God's people in need, raising funds to realize these ventures of faith and hope. And we plan to formulate and furnish the procedures, learned from our experiences at Koinonia, Losanganya, and Ntondo, to guide these new projects to completion.

This is a gigantic task. It calls for hundreds and hundreds of people committed to serving in the name of Christ—Baptists, Methodists, Lutherans, Presbyterians, Quakers, Mennonites, Disciples, United Church of Christ people, Episcopalians, Catholics, and many others. People of faith who are dedicated to activating their aspirations for a better world. People foolish enough to believe that God fully equips those who attempt great things for the Kingdom. People bold and unafraid to take risks, knowing that God has called us. People convinced that with God all things are possible.

We see this kind of ministry as an exciting new frontier in Christian missions. I personally believe it holds the future of the missionary enterprise.

The old days of traditional missionary activities—preaching, evangelizing, teaching, and healing—are fast coming to an end. On most mission fields today indigenous church leadership has replaced the missionaries in administration, pastoring local churches, and evangelistic work. Mission schools are being taken over by national governments—this happened in Zaire while we were there. Hospitals and other medical projects are increasingly coming under the domain of the state. In many countries we hear the cry, "Missionary, go home. Your work is over."

It is true that the day has come for the traditional missionary to go home. Those brave pioneers of the past made many mistakes, as we all do, but they played a tremendous and vital role in spreading the Christian gospel. They brought churches into being the world over, and they established thousands of schools, clinics, and hospitals. But the day of that approach is past. Now we must seek new ways to witness and minister in Christ's name.

Nor should we weep over these changes. I often think of the words of the dying King Arthur in Tennyson's famous poem:

> ... The old order changeth, yielding place to new;
> And God fulfills himself in many ways,
> Lest one good custom should corrupt the world.

Closed doors in one place mean open doors somewhere else. To serve the world as Christ's followers, we must simply find those newly opened doors and walk through them.

Pastor Lokoni already has pointed clearly to one of those doors.

"When the missionaries came many years ago," he said, "the first thing they did was to build nice houses for themselves. Next they built nice houses for God. But they didn't help the people build houses."

Projects like Losanganya and the one beginning at Ntondo literally capture the hearts of the people. A desperate need is filled, and in the process lines of communication are opened that otherwise often remain closed. Working together every day toward a common goal, you have countless opportunities to talk and share with people—ideas, aspirations, faith—while at the same time houses, backyard industries, gardens, and parks are emerging. You become deeply involved with people's lives. Every one of our volunteers lived with Zairois families in the development, sharing completely as a member of the household.

As we worked, all of us were caught up in the life of the church as well. Larry, Joe, and Cindy formed a musical group that sang regularly at church functions throughout the area. Linda joined Mama Beyeke's chorus and sang with them. I preached in countless church services, and Linda delivered the sermon on the Sunday in 1975 commemorating International Women's Year. I was also called upon to participate in a great many funerals, and these are always times which bring Christians close together.

With the housing project as the focal point of our work, we added the wooden leg and eyeglasses programs, Bible distribution, prison visitation, and community enrichment programs such as the sewing and cooking and nutrition and family planning classes run by Linda and Helen Weeks. In all these efforts we were able to make a significant impact on the lives of individuals.

These kinds of activities and programs are the substance of the new frontier. The door is open. The need is fantastic. We are invited, and I believe God is calling us to the task. It is an urgent one. As the colonial period has closed in Africa and elsewhere in the underdeveloped world, people have been thrown back on their own skills and resources. They are finding they cannot do the job alone. In Zaire, there has been much regression since independence. Prior to 1960, for example, the country was exporting a variety of agricultural products; now many of these same items must be imported. The standard of living has gone down as prices have skyrocketed. The cost of consumer goods in Mbandaka is now higher than in Washington, D.C. It has been said that Zaire could feed Africa—there is that much potential in this vast country. Instead, the people are not even adequately feeding themselves.

Can a world with an ever-increasing population, with attendant increasing needs for the necessities of life, continue to afford endless stretches of virtually unproductive land? I believe there is a real danger of recolonization in Africa and perhaps in other underdeveloped areas of the world if the people do not develop their countries and make them productive.

But how can poor, malnourished, uneducated, ill-housed people develop anything? How can they lift themselves up?

The answer is obvious: They cannot. They must have help from outside, and this help must be generous and total. Development is a multifaceted process. It must involve not only the land, but all the resources; not only agriculture and industry, but housing and community development as well; not only a few of the elite in a country, but all the people.

Who can do this job? Can it be left entirely to governments which make their decisions on the basis of political conditions?

Every day while we were in Zaire we were bombarded by Voice of America broadcasts announcing millions of dollars from the United States Government, the World Bank, and this or that governmental agency for development of Third World countries. But when we looked for the results of these tremendous grants and loans, they were hard to find. Certainly, few benefits filtered down to the very poor.

Can the job be left to businessmen, whose primary motivation is profit?

We have already seen that if Bokotola's residents had had to pay interest on top of their monthly house payments, the whole project would have had to be abandoned. And there is no way that the recipients of wooden legs and eyeglasses could have paid what these items cost to produce—even if they had been available in Mbandaka.

Despite all the inefficiencies and greed of governments and business, I realize they still have a big role to play in the overall growth process of underdeveloped countries. But they alone cannot do the job.

Churches and other organizations motivated by compassion, concern, and love must be heavily and increasingly involved. These groups, without political motivations or ambitions to make a profit, are free to help the people, to build *with* them. They can show the way, and at the same time they can serve as a conscience for others who are working in their spheres of activity.

In Mbandaka we were constantly aware that our efforts were being closely watched by both the local and national governments, and we observed our ideas and procedures being incorporated into their projects. We also saw local business interests taking note of what we were doing and being motivated to do something themselves to help the people.

The consequences of trying to ignore the tremendous problems confronting us are too awesome to even contemplate. If grinding poverty continues in these nations, with the population sitting idly on millions of acres of potentially useful land which produces virtually nothing, it is quite conceivable that some coldblooded politician in some overcrowded industrial nation will say, "Who needs those miserable people, anyway? Let's go down and wipe them out and turn that land into something valuable for *our* countrymen."

The world need is staggering, and our resources are pitifully small. There are too few concerned people. Frustrations—once you put your hand to the task—are on every side, created by inefficiency, negative attitudes, stupidity, and even open opposition from some of the people you seek to serve. But we know that with the power of God energizing us, small resources, few people, and big frustrations have a way of being taken care of. God has called us. We must do what we can with what we have, believing that with Him it will be sufficient for the task.

In our world of modern communications, we are well aware of the sad state of so many of our fellow human beings on this planet. The Jericho Road of today's world no longer starts in Jerusalem and ends in Jericho. It is much longer and wider now. It starts on one side of the town or city in which we live and goes out from there, passing through every country on earth. Finally it winds its way back, coming up behind us from the other side of our city until it connects with its starting point.

You are on that road, like it or not, and you have eyes that see. The question is whether you will walk by on the other side, away from where your neighbor is lying bleeding and suffering from all sorts of attacks. Attacks from bandits of hunger; a thousand worms in his belly; the despair of unemployment; a bloody infection for which there is no medicine; the rain and wind and cold that come through the walls of his miserable shack.

... Or whether, in the name of your common humanity and in the name of Christ, you will go to him, strengthened and guided by the spirit of the living God, and do what you can to help.

Epilogue

In September of 1976 a group of twenty-seven people from eleven states, plus Mompongo Mo Imana from Ntondo, Zaire, came together at Koinonia Farm for two days of intensive study, prayer, and brainstorming. We sought to answer the questions "Where do we go from here?" and "What is God calling us to do now?"

Emerging from that session was a unanimous feeling that God is calling us to continue unfolding the dream ... to ensure the completion of Losanganya and Ntondo, and to go on from there to wherever in the world He leads us ... to explore as fully as possible this new frontier in Christian mission.

A new organization, Habitat for Humanity, has been created to raise funds, recruit personnel, and provide procedures and expertise for developing proper "habitat" for God's children in need. We hope to inspire people everywhere to go to this new frontier and build with us to the glory of God.

Would you like to join us in this venture of faith? For information, write to: Habitat for Humanity, 417 W. Church Street, Americus, Georgia 31709.